WE ARE ~~DAUGHTERS~~
of Our
HEAVENLY FATHER

"*We Are Daughters of Our Heavenly Father* adds meaning and purpose with principles that are supported by carefully selected scriptures and relevant quotes from the Brethren, with significant examples that take the message off the page and into the heart of the reader as you read and digest the insightful message in this publication."

—Sister Ardeth G. Kapp, former
Young Women general president

"One of my favorite things about this book is that Jen speaks to young women in their own language. Not only that, but *We Are Daughters* is jam-packed with scriptures, stories, quotes, and insights that will draw any who read it closer to Christ. There's no doubt Jen's positive, energetic outlook will encourage and inspire young women of all ages."

—Jaci Wightman, author of *Body Image Breakthrough*

"Healthy introspection is a sure sign you're allowing all you do, hear, and say every Sunday to sink deep. Brewer's book helps trigger that sometimes uncomfortable and always enlightening journey of introspection for young (and older) women by starting in familiar territory. Just as the prophet Abraham's tests and trials helped "Abraham . . . learn something about Abraham" (see chapter 8), now's the perfect time to see your struggles with a broader view and move forward on that steep climb up your spiritual mountain to learn something new about you."

—Stacie Duce, *Mormon Times* columnist and magazine editor

"This book is a complete Young Women's package! With solid doctrine, excellent quotes, and appropriate personal experiences, young women will soak in the goodness. My favorite part? The thought-provoking questions—they're a built-in mother-daughter connection! When you add in the possible use for Personal Progress, you cannot enjoy a better Young Woman resource."

—Connie Sokol, mother of seven, bestselling author, national and local presenter

We Are
DAUGHTERS
of Our
HEAVENLY
FATHER

We Are DAUGHTERS of Our HEAVENLY FATHER

STRIVING to Live the YOUNG WOMEN VALUES

JEN BREWER

CFI
An Imprint of Cedar Fort, Inc.
Springville, Utah

ISBN 13: 978-1-4621-1673-7

Published by CFI, an imprint of Cedar Fort, Inc.
2373 W. 700 S., Springville, UT 84663
Distributed by Cedar Fort, Inc., www.cedarfort.com

LIBRARY OF CONGRESS CATALOGING-IN-PUBLICATION DATA

Brewer, Jen, 1974- author.
We are daughters of our Heavenly Father / Jen Brewer.
    pages cm
Includes bibliographical references.
ISBN 978-1-4621-1673-7
1. Young Women (Church of Jesus Christ of Latter-day Saints) 2. Mormon youth--Conduct of life. 3. Young women--Conduct of life. I. Title.

BX8643.Y6B746 2015
289.3'3208352--dc23

2015013331

Cover design by Shawnda T. Craig
Cover design © 2015 Lyle Mortimer
Edited and typeset by Jessica B. Ellingson

Printed in the United States of America

10 9 8 7 6 5 4 3 2 1

Printed on acid-free paper

To my three sweet daughters—Sarah, Elizabeth, and Anna.

And to the young women of the world:
May you always remember not only who you are
but also whose you are.

Contents

CONTENTS

Acknowledgments

*I*T IS SAID that many hands make light work. In the case of this book, many hands have made the whole writing, editing, and publishing completely possible. There is no way I could have done any of this without the help of many hands, and eyes, and keystroke help. My editors took what I dumped onto the computer and turned it into something more than I ever could have on my own. Whitney Archibald was a wiz at taking my initial scattered thoughts and arranging them into a much more presentable format. Lisa and Sadie Burt were a dynamic duo who questioned everything and made me reach down deeper than I ever thought I could. Sadie's "Points to Ponder" at the end of each chapter were sheer brilliance. Lisa Teixeira burned the midnight oil more than once in a last-run effort to cut out the extras and get to the guts of each subject. And of course, my soul sister Sue read way too many versions of this, as well as heard way too many exasperated sighs through the phone as she patiently reassured me it would all work out in the end. Jolene Reed's magic with the camera provided the perfect picture for the cover. I cherish her friendship and stand in awe at her creativity. Shawnda Craig's mad graphic design skills brought the cover together in a way that was absolutely magical.

Sister Ardeth Kapp Perry was so generous with her time and compliments as many phone calls and emails were exchanged in researching the history of the theme, as well as many other details throughout the book. Her enthusiasm and willingness to reach out has been invaluable.

ACKNOWLEDGMENTS

The whole team at Cedar Fort has been incredible through the final processes of getting this book to its final format. From editor Emily Chambers to copyeditor Jessica Ellingson, they have made the book what it is today.

And last, to Young Women leaders everywhere—including mine of yesteryear—thank you. Thank you for your patience, diligence, and steadfastness in keeping us true to the theme week after week and year after year as we all take our journeys through life into life eternal. Your efforts will never be forgotten!

LET'S START
at the
BEGINNING

We are daughters of our Heavenly Father, who loves us, and we love Him. We will "stand as witnesses of God at all times and in all things, and in all places" (Mosiah 18:9) as we strive to live the Young Women values, which are:

Faith

Divine Nature

Individual Worth

Knowledge

Choice and Accountability

Good Works

Integrity

and Virtue

We believe as we come to accept and act upon these values, we will be prepared to strengthen home and family, make and keep sacred covenants, receive the ordinances of the temple, and enjoy the blessings of exaltation.

—Young Women Theme

FROM THE TIME you turn twelve to your eighteenth birthday, you stand up every Sunday and recite these exact words. Every. Single. Sunday. Have you ever wondered why this theme was chosen? What in these paragraphs is so important that Heavenly Father wants to sear it into your brain, so much so that thirty-plus years down the road you will still be able to recall it at the drop of a hat? (Trust me, you will; it's still ingrained in my mind!) It's not—as I know some young women think—just something to get through each week so we can get to the "important" information.

Let's back up a bit—back to the beginning. The Young Women program was started by Brigham Young, as he called on his daughters to lead in a "retrenchment from the things of the world."[1] From its humble beginnings, the Young Women organization began growing and changing. There were many yearly themes instituted and different goal systems put into place to help the young women realize their full potential as daughters of God. Even the name of the organization changed throughout the years. (It was once called the "Young Ladies' Department of the Ladies' Cooperative Retrenchment Association"—quite a mouthful![2])

In 1984, Sister Ardeth G. Kapp was called as the general president of the Young Women. Sister Kapp, along with her presidency and the Young Women board, wanted to help the young women truly feel of their worth and importance as part of God's kingdom—not just as an auxiliary program but as an integral part of God's plan here on earth. The theme was a natural place for them to do this.

Instead of asking, "What do we want to do?" the presidency started with a goal-oriented question: "What do we want to have *happen*?" The answer was clear: for all young women to be prepared to receive the covenants and blessings of the temple.

They realized that at the end of the day, in all of the craziness of the world, there are two essential pillars that will never change: the covenants we make at the time of baptism, and those we make in the temple. They pondered and prayed for direction about how to help you as a young woman move along on the path from baptism to eternal temple covenants.

So began many days, weeks, and months of much fasting and prayer. Above all else, their constant heaven-sent plea was that the theme they wrote would indeed be God's will and vision for His daughters, something that would give the young women of the world a true sense of their identity, their duty, and their responsibilities as pure women of God.

The presidency met many times. They plastered papers on walls. They wrote, erased, and rewrote different phrases. At one point, the entire Young Women presidency and board went on a retreat, during which they all came together in fasting and prayer to focus specifically on what Heavenly Father would have them write.

In a world where people everywhere are clamoring for identity, they wanted to help *you* answer these basic questions: Who am I? What am I to do? Why do I need to do it? How do I do it?

As they pieced the theme together, the presidency continually pleaded with the Lord that if He accepted the theme, the Brethren's ears would be opened when the presidency presented it to their priesthood leaders, including the Apostles of the Church. But if the theme was not right, they prayed that the Brethren would let the sisters know so they could go back and keep working until it was what the Lord wanted. When the day came to present the theme to the Brethren, Elder David B. Haight, then a member of the Quorum of the Twelve Apostles, said, "Sisters, today you have not only opened our ears, but you have also opened our hearts."[3]

When Sister Kapp related this story to me, I felt chills. God truly does answer prayers. He answered Sister Kapp's prayers throughout the development of the theme. He will answer yours as you learn and live the theme.

Before we delve into the details, let's take a look at the theme in its entirety. One way to see it is to look at three main messages that are reiterated throughout the inspired sentences:

1. Who we are.
2. The responsibility we have to act and not to be acted upon.
3. The need to plan and prepare now for important decisions throughout our life.

All of these overarching ideas and concepts come to us in something that takes less than thirty seconds to recite each week!

Here's another underlying insight about the Young Women theme you may not have noticed: it is a succinct summary of the plan of salvation. While it doesn't specifically describe the Atonement and all the commandments, it includes the basic elements of the plan and answers the questions, "Where did I come from? Why am I here? Where am I going?" Further, the values tell you the basic hows, or attributes you need to develop, to get back to Heavenly Father. It is a perfect starting point to use when friends of other faiths have questions about who you are, what you believe, and why you keep the standards they see that are so different from the world.

Come with me on a journey. Let's slow things down and examine this theme. Let's cut it up line-by-line and really let the magnitude of the message sink into our hearts. As you go through each chapter, please take time to ponder and let the principles percolate inside you. Some of the ideas may sink deep. Other ideas may sting just a bit. Each chapter ending has a section set aside for you to stop and really think about how the principles pertain to you personally, and to write your thoughts, impressions, and goals as well.

Each of us comes from different circumstances in life. You may come from an ideal Latter-day Saint home, raised by an active mother and father who are there to walk with you every step. You may come from a single-parent home. You may be the only member in your entire family, with less-than-supportive surroundings. Rather than use your circumstances to discount the principles discussed in this book, reflect on your inner struggles and evaluate yourself. Let your questions guide your studies as you seek to truly ingrain the message of the Young Women theme into your heart and mind, and permit it to help you in your personal circumstances, whatever they may be.

Chapter 2

WE ARE DAUGHTERS
of Our
HEAVENLY FATHER

IOLOGICALLY, SOME OF us are sisters. We may be cousins, aunts, or nieces. We are hoping to one day be wives and mothers. But first, we are daughters. And before we were daughters of our earthly fathers, we were daughters of our Heavenly Father.

I don't know if I can truly explain the utter, engulfing love that comes over someone who holds his or her baby for the first time. It is real. It is all-encompassing. It is all about that fresh, pure spirit. Think of what that might feel like. Ask your mom or dad to tell you about the time they first held you in their arms. Then multiply that feeling by infinity. *That* is how much you mean to our Heavenly Father. *You are His daughter.* Above all else, never forget that.

Years ago the Quorum of the Twelve Apostles reminded us of this intimate relationship when they stated, "It is significant that of all the titles of respect and honor and admiration that are given to Deity, He has asked us to address Him as Father."[1]

He is your Father. He wants you to come back to heaven with Him—back home. At the end of the day, that's *all* He wants—to have us come home to Him (see Moses 1:39). He is expecting us.

Can you feel it? Can you feel the hug that is waiting for you just on the other side of the veil?

Years ago—back in the "olden days," as my kids would say—I was just finishing up my mission in Guatemala. My father was serving as a mission president in Mexico, just bordering my mission. So my grand return home was to Mexico. I remember getting on the last plane and thinking how different this was going to be compared to the normal welcome home parties I had witnessed at airports growing up, where an entire crowd is gathered with posters, balloons, and tons of people to greet the returning missionaries.

What I experienced instead will forever leave an impression on my soul. I made my way out of the plane and through the gate and then walked through a long corridor, at the end of which people were lined up to greet the passengers. I scanned the crowd and quickly found my parents. As I reached them, my dad swooped me into the biggest hug I can ever remember receiving from him. We sat there, both of us frozen in time, tears streaming down our cheeks, as he excitedly whispered into my ear, "You did it! You made it! And now you're back!"

I have reflected on this incident over and over through the years. When we finish our earthly missions, I am quite certain our return will be similar. Can you imagine that? Think of it—being scooped up into that all-engulfing heavenly hug by your Eternal Father, whom you will recognize instantly. President Brigham Young described it this way:

> There is no spirit but what was pure and holy when it came here from the celestial world. . . . He is the Father of our spirits; and if we could know, understand, and do His will, every soul would be prepared to return back into His presence. And when they get there, they will see that they had formerly lived there for ages, that they had previously been acquainted with every nook and corner, with the palaces, walks, and gardens; and they would embrace their Father, and He would embrace them and say, "My son, my daughter, I have you again;" and the child would say, "Oh my Father, my Father, I am here again.'[2]

The prophet Alma also testified of this: "Behold, it has been made known unto me by an angel, that the spirits of all men, as soon as they are departed from this mortal body, yea, the spirits of all men, whether they be good or evil, are taken home to that God who gave them life" (Alma 40:11).

Isn't that such a comforting thought that when we die we get to go back home, to our Father, to that God who gave us life. I can't wait for that Father hug.

Yes, He is your father. *You* are His daughter.

POINTS TO PONDER FROM CHAPTER 2

You may choose to ponder and pray about each concept as you answer the questions below. Plan how you can strengthen and build your testimony and act upon the principles you have studied.

How can I know for myself that I am a daughter of God?

_____
_____
_____
_____

How will I act, knowing I have a divine inheritance?

_____
_____
_____
_____

How will understanding who I am help me determine my choices?

_____
_____
_____
_____

What does being a daughter of God mean to me?

_____

_____

_____

_____

    For further insight, study Alma 40 and Moses 1. Consider how our Heavenly Father addresses Moses.

Chapter 3

WHO LOVES US

THIS IS HOW much He loves you: Your Father in Heaven wants you home so badly that He gave you a big Brother, Jesus Christ. Then He let your Brother suffer and die so that His sons and His daughters could live. So *you* could live. And not just live—so you could live *eternally* with Him.

Your Father did that for you. And He asked *nothing* in return as payment to Him. Instead, what He requires of us is to keep His commandments (Mosiah 2:22). But that's just a way of saying that He wants us to stay safe and return to Him. Can we really count that as something we are doing for Him? When we keep His commandments, as King Benjamin explains, then He immediately blesses us, so we are still indebted to Him (Mosiah 2:24). We can never get one up on God; He will always pay us more than we deserve because we will always be imperfect as mortals. I don't say that to downplay the challenge of trying to keep the commandments. Let's just be honest; it's hard to keep all of the commandments all of the time. The point that I'm trying to make with this is that our keeping the commandments is not paying off our Debtor—God. Keeping the commandments is really for our benefit, as well as to prove our obedience and learn to become like Christ, which is why we were sent to earth as part of the plan of salvation.

Have you ever felt insignificant? Have you ever been in a big group of people and felt so small—so utterly alone—like no one even knew you existed? There are over seven billion people on the earth right now. That's a lot of people with whom to compete for attention. In the whole grand scheme of things, we really are nothing. In fact, we are even lower than the dust of the earth, because even the dust of the earth obeys God's every command (Helaman 12:7–8).

And yet, somehow, with all the billions of people on earth, He knows *you*. More than that, He *loves* you. He loves you so much that if you were the only person on earth, He still would have allowed your Brother to suffer in Gethsemane. He did it for everyone. For every *one*. For *you*. C. S. Lewis put it like this: "[God] has infinite attention to spare for each one of us. He does not have to deal with us in the mass. You are as much alone with Him as if you were the only being He had ever created. When Christ died, He died for you individually just as much as if you had been the only man [or woman] in the world."[1]

This is such a simple concept to understand as far as it pertains to everyone; it's easy for many of us to testify that of course He loves His children . . . in the mass. For some of us, it becomes a much more difficult concept to actually believe and internalize, "He loves *me*." Alone. Without anyone else—or anything else—involved: no makeup, no money, no hair color. That God truly loves me, {insert your name}, unconditionally and eternally is where it gets personal.

I have been through this. I remember a time during my girls' camp years when we had a devotional about the love of God. I believed it. I knew that He loved His children. But as I looked around, I just couldn't comprehend that He would even know my name, let alone love me, personally.

One of our leaders counseled us to go to a spot in the mountains at some point during our alone time and say a prayer out loud, asking God if He was there. She said that she knew He would speak to us, that we would hear it. I got so excited about this. If He would answer my prayer specifically, then that would mean He knew me individually, that He loved me individually. With much anticipation, I almost ran to a secluded spot in the mountains. I said the prayer. I listened. I didn't hear anything. I said it again. Still nothing. After a bit of time, I reasoned that He was probably too busy to answer me right then; after all, there were a lot of girls at camp that week, and if He was answering everyone, maybe He just didn't have time to get to me. I remember not wavering in my testimony of God's love for us, collectively. I just didn't think I was that important for Him to spend His time answering little ol' me, individually. And this feeling stayed with me for years.

Looking back, how sad I am that I didn't realize *how* God answers me. It took some time in my life before I started to realize a pattern in how God answers my prayers. It is so individual and so specifically scripted to me that it undeniably proves to me that He does indeed know and love *me*, individually. It just took me tuning my spiritual ears to recognize it.

One such time happened when I was walking the trails of a mountain range in the middle of Guatemala. It was right in the middle of my mission, and I was struggling. I wasn't getting along quite right with my companion, and I was feeling discouraged because people were not grasping this incredibly glorious news of the gospel. I knew I couldn't really reach out to anyone of my close family or friends for help. And, because it wasn't preparation day, I couldn't write any letters. Of course, it wasn't Mother's Day or Christmas, so I couldn't make any phone calls to my parents either. For the first time in my life, I felt truly and utterly alone—less than a speck on this overwhelmingly large planet of ours. Then this quote from Abraham Lincoln came to mind: "I have been driven many times upon my knees by the overwhelming conviction that I had nowhere else to go."[2]

That night, I knelt down and had what I called my "hate prayer" with God. I let down all of my walls. I let go of trying to say, "Thank you for these trials." I poured out everything in my heart to Him. And some of those things were not very warm or fuzzy.

At the end of my prayer, I fully expected either nothing or a lightning bolt to come (knowing that I certainly deserved it for some of the thoughts I had actually expressed to Him!). What I received instead will forever remain with me—yet another moment of confirmation that He loves me, alone, without all the pomp and circumstance. He loved me even when I was my most raw self. I didn't hear anything; I didn't see any flashing lights. But what I felt, I will never forget. It was as if I could feel Him enter my head as I thought this phrase: "Finally. Finally you have come to me. You are not here to do this alone. You *can't* do this alone. But with me, you can do anything. You are my daughter, and if you are hurting, I am here for you." I felt the biggest spiritual hug I have ever encountered. It took me so off guard and was so profound that I almost didn't know what to say. But I had to keep talking so the feeling wouldn't go away! I remember talking about anything and everything just to keep Him right there with me.

I have come to put a borrowed label on these experiences. In April 2005, Elder David A. Bednar spoke about the "tender mercies" that are continually extended to each and every one of us (1 Nephi 1:20). He taught us that tender mercies "are the very personal and individualized blessings, strength, protection, assurances, guidance, loving-kindnesses, consolation, support, and spiritual gifts which we receive from and because of and through the Lord Jesus Christ."[3]

Tender mercies are, to me, the ultimate exemplification of God's individual love for each and every one of us. I have found in my life, when I am feeling far away from God, that if I simply take out a pen and paper and start to list the tender mercies I have seen in my life, even in the past few days, I am profoundly brought back to the personal and detailed love He shows me on a daily basis.

If you are feeling far from God, or just feeling insignificant in the universe, give it a try. Simply try to find one tender mercy that you have seen in your life in the past little while. It doesn't have to be grand or glorious. In fact, for me, the beauty of the tiny tender mercies is that it shows not only His individualized love for each of us, but also just how intimately He knows us, and therefore knows how to succor us in the small, almost imperceptible ways. For Elder Bednar, previous to his first general conference address, it was a hymn that was sung just before he spoke.[4]

When you do write down those tender mercies, take a moment to realize that tender mercies do not always help us *out* of trials in our lives. Oftentimes, they are the things that help us *through* the trials in our lives (Mosiah 24).

You are so loved! President Uchtdorf expressed the beauty of God's love for you in October 2014. He reminded us that God doesn't wait until we reach a certain point on our road to perfection. He stated, "He loves you today with a full understanding of your struggles. . . . He knows of the times you have held onto the fading light and believed—even in the midst of growing darkness. He knows of your sufferings. He knows of your remorse for the times you have fallen short or failed. *And still He loves you.*"[5]

I end this chapter with an invitation extended from one of the great Book of Mormon prophets, Jacob. He invites us all to "lift up [our] heads and . . . feast upon [Christ's] love" (Jacob 3:2). His love is there. It is eternal. And it is for you.

POINTS TO PONDER FROM CHAPTER 3

You may choose to ponder and pray about each concept as you answer the questions below. Plan how you can strengthen and build your testimony and act upon the principles you have studied.

Where in the scriptures are verses or accounts that portray God's love for His children as individuals?

_____
_____
_____
_____
_____
_____
_____
_____

How has God shown His love for me as a unique daughter?

_____
_____
_____
_____
_____
_____
_____
_____

How can I know for myself that God loves me, personally?

_____
_____
_____
_____
_____
_____
_____
_____

Why does God love us? Why does He love me?

_____
_____
_____
_____
_____
_____
_____
_____

WE ARE DAUGHTERS OF OUR HEAVENLY FATHER

How does the Lord help us through the adversity we experience? How do we access the power of the Atonement when it is not redemption but comfort we seek?

_____
_____
_____
_____
_____
_____
_____
_____

What will I do to remember to watch for God's love on a daily basis?

_____
_____
_____
_____
_____
_____
_____

For further insight on God's love, compassion, and mercy in regards to His children, see Mosiah 24; Moses 7:20–34, 37, 39–40. See also:

- M. Russell Ballard, "The Atonement and the Value of One Soul," *Ensign*, May 2004;
- David A. Bednar, "The Tender Mercies of the Lord," *Ensign*, May 2005;
- Jeffrey R. Holland, "'He Loved Them unto the End,'" *Ensign*, November 1989;
- Brad Wilcox, "His Grace Is Sufficient," BYU Speeches, July 12, 2011;
- Terryl and Fiona Givens, *The God Who Weeps: How Mormonism Makes Sense of Life* (Salt Lake City: Deseret Book, 2013).

Chapter 4

AND WE LOVE HIM

W HEN JESUS WAS questioned by the Pharisees and Sadducees what the great commandment was, He answered simply, "Thou shalt love the Lord thy God with all thy heart, and with all thy soul, and with all thy mind" (Matthew 22:37). Why do you think this is so important, and why is it the first thing Jesus listed? Marvin J. Ashton, then a member of the Quorum of the Twelve Apostles, related something he learned from a taxi driver long ago: "That which we love will be that to which we give our allegiance."[1] If we love something, we naturally want to focus on it and put it first in our lives. In Exodus, we learn that the first commandment Moses brought down from Mount Sinai was, "Thou shalt have no other gods before me" (Exodus 20:3).

It may seem easy to put a check mark next to this commandment since we obviously aren't bowing down to golden cows or other idols, as did the children of Israel when this commandment was first given. However, Elder Dallin H. Oaks of the Quorum of the Twelve Apostles gave an interesting label to "other gods" in modern times. He referred to them as priorities. He counseled us to seriously consider the priorities we have in our lives and ask ourselves if we are placing (or serving) other priorities over God. He made some specific suggestions including "cultural or family traditions, political correctness, career aspirations, material possessions, recreational pursuits," just to name a few.[2] A short time later, Elder Russell M. Nelson added to this list by asking if we placed our faith in sports teams or celebrities more than in God.[3]

Are there areas in your life where you are placing other priorities ahead of God? Fitting in with the right social group? Pursuing the cutest boyfriend? Searching for just the right "selfie" to post on Facebook instead of reading the scriptures? The list could go on, but the principle remains the same: having social, physical, or other interests in life is not breaking the first commandment; when those priorities come before our love of God and following His ways, then we break the commandment.

To bring it back to the beginning, I trust that you do love God. It is natural to love someone who loves us first. The more you come to know your Father in Heaven, the more you come to feel His love. The more you feel His love, the more you are filled with love for Him in return. This love then becomes evident in the choices we make each day as we obey or disobey His laws.

It is easy to *say* that we love someone, but what do we *do* if we love someone? What if we acted on the love, not just passively said the words? Jesus also answered this question for us: "If ye love me, keep my commandments" (John 14:15).

Think of what a different world we would see if people simply abided by the Ten Commandments. Years ago, Ted Koppel, a famous news anchor, gave a brilliant speech in which he stated, "What Moses brought down from Mt. Sinai were not the Ten Suggestions—they are Commandments. *Are*, not *were*."[4]

Truly a whole book could be written on the fact that the Ten Commandments are just as pertinent to us today as they were when Moses first walked down from the mountain. Instead, I will defer to the *For the Strength of Youth* pamphlet, which perfectly summarizes not only how applicable the commandments still are, but also tells us in specific ways just how we can apply them in our lives.[5]

What I would like to focus on is *keeping* the commandments, or being obedient to God.

There are three levels of obedience. The first is motivated by fear. At age three, we don't really know *why* we stay out of the street; we just know Mom gets really mad when we run into it! In other words, we are obedient to our parents because they are our parents. Then comes the next level: we obey because we understand the consequences of not obeying. In other words, we come to understand that if we run into the street, a car could hit us.

There is a third level, in which we obey out of love. To go back to the street example, we start to realize we love our parents and they love us, and we want to do everything in our power to stay safe and be able to stay together as a family. So not only do we not go into the street, but we also obey other traffic and safety rules as well. We have a desire to obey; our will has changed.

That third level of obedience doesn't come all at once. It comes as we learn of Christ, believe in Christ, and have our hearts changed by Christ. When we have "experienced this mighty change in [our] hearts" (Alma 5:14), a natural outpouring of our expression of love is to have no more desire to do evil (see Mosiah 5:2; Mosiah 18; Moroni 7:13; Ether 8:26).

President Dieter F. Uchtdorf explains, "Love is the measure of our faith, the inspiration for our obedience, and the true altitude of our discipleship."[6] Obedience is a natural outgrowth of love.

Is it okay to obey out of the first two levels? Absolutely. The sheer act of obedience will help us to progress along the levels, from simply doing to being. In other words, as we practice obedience just because we know we should, we grow to understand the why, our love for God grows, and we become changed on the inside. It is a beautiful cycle—one that can help us cultivate our love for God. As our obedience grows, so does our love for God, which in turn will help us to want to be even more obedient.

No one ever said obedience would be easy. Even when we do love God with all of our hearts, obeying is still hard at times, but that doesn't mean we love God less. What matters is that we work past our own natural-man instincts and truly "becometh as a child, submissive, meek, humble, patient, full of love, willing to submit to all things which the Lord seeth fit to inflict upon him, even as a child doth submit to his father" (Mosiah 3:19). Even Christ felt some of this inner turmoil as He walked to perform the greatest act of our salvation: His Atonement. He literally "fell on his face, and prayed, saying, O my Father, if it be possible, let this cup pass from me" (Matthew 26:39). Yes, obedience can be very trying at times, as even our Savior experienced. But the important point is that we can rise above our own instincts and truly come to show our love through our actions, as did Christ: "Nevertheless not as I will, but as thou wilt" (Matthew 26:39).

In the end, God truly does not *need* us to love Him; He didn't give us "the first and great commandment" (Matthew 22:38) for His benefit. If we disregard Him, His power is not diminished in any way. As President Uchtdorf explains: "His influence and dominion extend through time and space independent of our acceptance, approval, or admiration." He goes on to admonish, "No, God does not need us to love Him. But oh, how we need to love God! For what we love determines what we seek. What we seek determines what we think and do. What we think and do determines who we are—and who we will become."[7]

Yes, our choosing to love God is something that will truly help us become like Him and engrave His image in our countenances (Alma 5:19).

POINTS TO PONDER FROM CHAPTER 4

You may choose to ponder and pray about each concept as you answer the questions below. Plan how you can strengthen and build your testimony and act upon the principles you have studied.

How do I show my love for God?

_____
_____
_____
_____

WE ARE DAUGHTERS OF OUR HEAVENLY FATHER

At what level(s) of obedience do I follow the Lord's commandments? How will I change my motivation to obey?

_____
_____
_____
_____
_____
_____
_____
_____

Do I put other priorities ahead of obeying the Lord? What are they, and how will I change?

_____
_____
_____
_____
_____
_____
_____
_____

How can I help my family members choose the right?

_____
_____
_____
_____
_____
_____
_____
_____

For further insight on showing your love to God, see the following references:

- Marvin J. Ashton, "We Serve That Which We Love," *Ensign*, May 1981;
- Dallin H. Oaks, "No Other Gods," *Ensign*, November 2013;
- Russell M. Nelson, "Let Your Faith Show," *Ensign*, May 2014;
- Dieter F. Uchtdorf, "The Love of God," *Ensign*, November 2009.

Chapter 5

WE WILL
Stand as Witnesses
OF GOD

WHAT DOES IT mean to be a witness? One type of witness stands up in court. He or she has the power to convict. If you are the witness of a car accident, a crime, or any event, it means that you saw it or heard it. You have your own personal account of what happened. Will you share this with others? Will you deny it?

Have you witnessed enough of God's love and His hand in your life that you can truly stand as a witness of Him? I would submit that you have. If you look for it, He is everywhere. As discussed in chapter three, His tender mercies surround you each and every day (see 1 Nephi 1:14, 20; Psalm 119:77).[1] Once we receive a witness (or testimony), it becomes incumbent upon us to stand for that witness.

If you think about family units, part of what family members (hopefully) do is stand up for each other. As a daughter of God and part of an eternal family, you are to stand up and stand tall for Him. In fact, so important is standing as a witness that after His resurrection, when Jesus ministered to His disciples for forty days, His final words to them were, "Ye shall be witnesses unto me . . . unto the uttermost part of the earth" (Acts 1:8).

If we go back and look at the big picture of the theme, this is one example of acting instead of being acted upon. Standing up takes action. Sometimes, standing will help others to stand also. Other times, you will indeed stand alone. President Monson reminded us it wouldn't always be easy: "As we go about living from day to day, it is almost inevitable that our faith will be challenged."[2]

Many of us have deep convictions, some of which are not popular with the current social status quo. Yet how many of us are brave enough to stand up (yes, even stand alone) and make our convictions known? I know that it is hard for me to do this at times, especially when I feel like the whole room around me is in unified agreement on the opposite side of the spectrum. It takes a lot of guts to act.

Even when we do act, we will not always be congratulated. We may at times be ridiculed. Some people have even been thrown in jail, like Joseph in Egypt. He stood as a witness against Potiphar's wife, and as a result he was thrown in prison (Genesis 39:9, 20). Abinadi stood as a witness and ended up being put to death (Mosiah 17). Shadrach, Meshach, and Abed-nego stood as witnesses against the great King Nebuchadnezzar and were thrown into a fiery furnace (Daniel 3:12–23). Esther was asked to stand as a witness against one of the kings most trusted servants at the peril of her own life (Esther 4:10–14; 7:2–6).

Sometimes we may feel like our standing up is all in vain. We may feel like the instant results are the only results. Let's revisit the outcomes of the previous examples. Joseph, by interpreting and giving counsel regarding Pharaoh's dream, became the second in power behind Pharaoh in Egypt and saved not only the people of Egypt but also his own family (Genesis 41:14–43; 45:3–18). Abinadi had one convert from his standing as a witness (which he most likely never even knew about while he was alive). That one convert, Alma the Elder, taught others, and hundreds were converted (Mosiah 18:10–16), leading to an entire nation of people who came to know the true principles of Christ.

Shadrach, Meshach, and Abed-nego humbly told King Nebuchadnezzar that they didn't know if God would deliver them, but even if they were to die, they would not shrink from standing as a witness (Daniel 3:15–18). The result? Not only were they saved, but we are also told that not one hair on their heads was burned. They didn't even have the campfire smell on them (Daniel 3:27)! King Nebuchadnezzar then actually promoted them in his kingdom (Daniel 3:30). They went from being condemned to death to being promoted. Finally, Esther saved not only the life of her uncle, but also the lives of her entire people (Esther 8:2, 11).

We most likely will not be called to stand before kings or face death for standing up for our beliefs. We may not even be called to appear before huge groups in monumental calls for our witness of God. But make no mistake, our standing as a witness in our group of friends, in our homes, or in our schools is just as vital. No act is too small.

The question is, once you receive the witness of God in your life, are you willing to stand for Him? Will people be able to know God because they know you? Or will you hide your witness? We need to stand, not shrink from the witness of Heavenly Father. He tells us distinctly that we need to stand tall. He taught the Jews and later the Nephites in America the counsel to "let your light so shine before this people, that they may see your good works and *glorify your Father who is in heaven*" (3 Nephi 12:16; emphasis added; see also Matthew 5:16). We want to stand up and stand out—not so *we* stand up and stand out, but so He does.

You are a witness just by your example. When you refuse to lower your standards in how you dress, you are standing as a witness. When you choose to use clean language, you are standing as a witness. When you uphold the law of chastity, you are standing as a witness. And your friends are watching. Sister Nadauld, former general Young Women's president, taught us that even being kind is indeed standing as a witness. "Standing as a witness . . . means being kind in all things, being the first to say hello, being the first to smile, being the first to make the stranger feel a part of things, being helpful, thinking of others' feelings, being inclusive."[3]

You have a light. You may not see it, but other people do. They see that light in your eyes. Years ago, President Ezra Taft Benson and Elder Jeffrey R. Holland traveled to Jerusalem to secure land for a building to house BYU students studying abroad there. In order to get the permit, they had to sign a contract stating that there would be no proselyting by anyone using the building. After signing the contract, someone said, "Oh, we know that you are not going to proselyte, but what are you going to do about the light that is in their eyes?"[4]

Yes, you have a light. Don't hide it under a bushel. Stand up. Stand out. Stand as a witness of God!

POINTS TO PONDER FROM CHAPTER 5

You may choose to ponder and pray about each concept as you answer the questions below. Plan how you can strengthen and build your testimony and act upon the principles you have studied.

What does it mean to "stand as a witness of God"?

_____

_____

_____

_____

_____

_____

_____

_____

How does my behavior accurately reflect what I believe?

_____

_____

_____

_____

_____

_____

_____

What will I change in my conduct to "let [my] light so shine"?

_____

_____

_____

_____

_____

_____

_____

_____

Why does it matter that I stand as a witness of God always?

_____

_____

_____

_____

_____

_____

_____

How will I stand as a witness of God always to my family? To my friends? At school? At work? On dates? To my future children?

_____

_____

_____

_____

_____

_____

_____

How and with whom can I share the gospel now?

_____

_____

_____

_____

_____

_____

_____

For further insight on standing as a witness of God, see Job 13:8. See also:

- Jeffrey R. Holland, "The First Great Commandment," *Ensign*, November 2012;
- Neil L. Andersen, "Spiritual Whirlwinds," *Ensign*, May 2014;
- James E. Faust, "The Light in Their Eyes," *Ensign*, November 2005;
- Richard C. Edgley, "The Rescue for Real Growth," *Ensign*, May 2012;
- Thomas S. Monson, "Dare to Stand Alone," *Ensign*, November 2011;
- Margaret D. Nadauld, "Stand as a Witness," *Ensign*, May 2000.

Chapter 6

AT ALL TIMES
and in All Things,
AND IN ALL PLACES

You are an example—always—whether you know it or not. You don't get to decide when and where you want to be an example. The question is, what kind of example are you? Elder Jeffrey R. Holland counseled us, "Lesson number one for the establishment of Zion in the 21st century: You never 'check your religion at the door.' Not ever. My young friends, that kind of discipleship cannot be—it is not discipleship at all."[1]

You don't check your religion at the door. That means you represent your values *everywhere* you go. All places. Not just in Church meetings. Everywhere. At school. On the bus. At the dance. At the movies. Even in your own bedroom.

There are so many bad movies out there. Why? Because we are going to them! How many people are uncomfortable while watching them? Why don't we take a stand and get up and leave? The film industry would get the hint pretty quickly if people followed their gut and left or, better yet, didn't go at all. The market for these raunchy movies, I think, is not so much because people actually like them, but because people are too scared to stand up and stand out.

Don't be just a Sunday Saint. Be a Weekday Warrior! We need to be at the battlefront and ready to go 24/7. There is no time to take it easy.

Toward the end of his life, President Kimball took a trip to Bolivia with other General Authorities to meet with the Saints there and speak at many of their regional conferences. He worked at a non-stop pace, constantly greeting individual members and staying after meetings to speak with them. Others were taking breaks to get oxygen to try to acclimate (they were at an altitude of twelve thousand feet). Dr. Wilkinson, who had accompanied the General Authorities, finally approached and asked President Kimball if he would like to take a break soon to regain his energy. President Kimball responded, "If you knew what I knew, you wouldn't ask me that question."[2] I have often wondered what it was that President Kimball knew that kept him working at *all* times and in *all* places.

What about "all things"? Why not just "at all times . . . and in all places"? What does it mean to be a witness in *all things*? How we dress? How we act? How we socialize? How we use the Internet? Sister Nadauld gave an answer to this by stating, "Standing as a witness in all things means *all* things—big things, little things, in all conversations, in jokes, in games played and books read and music listened to, in causes supported, in service rendered, in clothes worn, in friends made."[3] *All things.* Yes, it even means online. You cannot hide behind the anonymous persona of the Internet. There is no such thing as anonymity with Heavenly Father.

Think of a time when you felt really uncomfortable. Have you ever been in a class where you felt totally lost but were too embarrassed to ask a question or make it known that you were not getting it? When some brave soul finally asked the question, do you remember how relieved you were that the person asked it? Or do you remember how relieved you were that someone else suggested another movie or another song?

Sometimes you will be the one who helps others to stand too; you'll be an example for them as they make decisions now or in the future. They may think back on your actions and choose differently because of you. They will look up to you and respect you for respecting your standards.

Be that someone. Be willing to *stand* as a witness, not just sit and stew. Be an agent to act, not a passive object to be acted upon.[4] *Do* something. Stand up and let your voice be heard. *Be* the change that needs to happen in your circles.

One young woman, Sarah, was not yet twelve years old and just starting sixth grade. During the first week of school, she found herself faced with a dilemma. One of her teachers ended the class each day by reading a book out loud to the students. It was a great book, but there were many swear words in it, which the teacher repeated out loud as she read the book. Sarah felt more and more uncomfortable as it became apparent that the swear words were not going to slow down anytime during the course of the book. She felt strange, wondering what this new teacher would think of her complaining within the first week of meeting her. After class, she humbly approached the teacher and explained that though she liked the book, the swear words made her feel uncomfortable, and she especially didn't like hearing them out loud. The teacher thanked her and no longer repeated swear words in any books for the rest of the year. It was a relatively small act by the world's standards; there was no fanfare, and no big cheers came from the other classmates. The teacher did not suddenly become interested in the gospel and get baptized. But Sarah learned that if she stood strong for her beliefs and her witness of Christ, she could indeed change her world for the better.

Be the student who stands up for the right. I guarantee you are not the only uncomfortable person. Don't let people mistake your silence for compliance. If you are uncomfortable, *say it*. Stand up!

POINTS TO PONDER FROM CHAPTER 6

You may choose to ponder and pray about each concept as you answer the questions below. Plan how you can strengthen and build your testimony and act upon the principles you have studied.

JEN BREWER

Write your testimony here:

_____
_____
_____
_____
_____
_____
_____
_____

What are God's standards?

_____
_____
_____
_____
_____
_____
_____
_____

What do I need to change in my life to better "stand as a witness of God at all times and in all things, and in all places"? (Consider movies, TV, Facebook, your language and conversation, music, and dress.)

_____
_____
_____
_____
_____
_____
_____

WE ARE DAUGHTERS OF OUR HEAVENLY FATHER

How do I already "stand as a witness of God at all times and in all things, and in all places" for the gospel of Jesus Christ?

_____
_____
_____
_____
_____
_____
_____
_____

How can I help others live the Lord's standards?

_____
_____
_____
_____
_____
_____
_____

For more insight on being a disciple of Christ always, see Romans 1:16 and *For the Strength of Youth*. See also:
- Jeffrey R. Holland, "Israel, Israel, God Is Calling," CES Devotional, September 9, 2012;
- Robert D. Hales, "Examples from the Life of a Prophet," *Ensign*, November 1981;
- David A. Bednar, *Increase in Learning: Spiritual Patterns for Obtaining Your Own Answers* (Salt Lake City: Deseret Book, 2011);
- David A. Bednar, *Act in Doctrine: Spiritual Patterns for Turning from Self to the Savior* (Salt Lake City: Deseret Book, 2012), especially Chapter 2: "Acting in Doctrine and Moral Agency," pages 36–73.

Chapter 7

AS WE STRIVE
to Live the
YOUNG WOMEN VALUES

ONCE SISTER KAPP and the rest of the Young Women presidency and board had the first part of the theme mapped out, they wondered about what specifically would help you as a young woman on your road back home to your Father in Heaven. Goals had long since been a part of the Young Women program—goals that were aimed at helping you reach your full potential here on the earth.

But they drew a distinction between goals and values. Temporal goals can change as the days and years go by. Values, on the other hand, are the unchanging, stalwart pillars upon which lives and hearts can be anchored. The values they chose, if internalized, would need to truly help young women become unchangeable and unstoppable women of God.

To determine what values to include, the presidency went back to the scriptures in fasting and prayer. They carefully studied and pondered which one should come first and why. Slowly, the list of values emerged.

It's interesting to me that the theme doesn't just say *learn* the values; it says *live* them. Internalize them. Ingrain them in your heart. Even more, engrave them into your bones.

The history of the song "I Am a Child of God" teaches us a valuable lesson in the difference between learning and living. Naomi Randall wrote the iconic children's hymn in 1957. For several years, the chorus read, "Teach me all that I must *know* to live with Him someday." Spencer W. Kimball, then a member of the Quorum of the Twelve Apostles, was visiting a stake conference where the children sang the beloved song. On his way home, he said, "I love the children's song, but there is one word that bothers me. Would Sister Randall mind if the word *know* were changed to the word *do*?" She agreed, and the song has been that way ever since.[1] It teaches us that in order to gain eternal life, knowing is not enough; we must *do*. Don't just learn the values. *Live* them.

The values are not simply a checklist of to-do items that you can cross off and then go about the rest of your activities. The process of doing the activities associated with the values in the Personal Progress program is more than just a speed-through-to-finish assignment. It's a pathway you can use to make the change from *doing* to *being*. This is actually where the road gets a bit fuzzy: Do we do the value goals because we have internalized the values, or do we internalize the values because we do them? I submit to you that it is a cycle (much like the obedience and love cycle in chapter four). In the doing, we become, which in turn makes the doing easier.

Elder Lynn G. Robbins of the Seventy gave a great talk regarding this cyclical process in 2011. He taught us, "To be and to do are inseparable. As interdependent doctrines they reinforce and promote each other. Faith inspires one to pray, for example, and prayer in turn strengthens one's faith." He further explains that to *do* without *being* denotes hypocrisy, and to *be* without *doing* isn't really being at all; it's actually only deceiving ourselves.[2]

Please don't misunderstand. Like stated previously, there is a process to this principle. There is room for testing and trying the doctrine (see John 7:17) as you grow into the *being* through the acts of *doing*. One of the best ways to come to love the commandments is to first live the commandments. This is something that can be worked on together. In other words, we don't have to dissect which comes first, the doing or the being; we can actually work on both simultaneously.

In fulfilling your value goals, many of you will undoubtedly create to-do lists. Yet how many of us have created *to-be* lists for ourselves? And what exactly are we to be like? Christ Himself gave us that answer when He appeared among the Nephites and told them, "What manner of men ought ye to be? Verily I say unto you, even as I am" (3 Nephi 27:27). In that same visit, He also told them, "That which ye have seen me do even that shall ye do" (3 Nephi 27:21).

Are you a bit overwhelmed with all of this doing and being, and working and becoming talk? Take a breath. Step back. And remember that this happens one step at a time. God reminds us multiple times throughout the scriptures, "Line upon line, precept upon precept" (D&C 98:12) and "here a little and there a little" (2 Nephi 28:30; see also Isaiah 28:10, 13). It starts with the small things. It starts with where you are right now. Then you take a step. You act. You begin to feel. Then you take another. Soon you are feeling and acting simultaneously, and the effort becomes part of you.

You may not have the greatest testimony of each of the values, but you have been taught that it is the best way to live. Great! Start there. Start doing the things your parents and leaders counsel you to do through Personal Progress. As you do the items (the checklists), really take some time to stop and internalize how these activities make you feel inside. Start to notice small changes that occur inside you. Act upon them to reinforce the changes and make them part of who you are.

It may be imperceptible at first. You may think you feel nothing. Be patient. Look to the Lord. He will work inside you, if you will let Him in. You are showing your trust in Him simply by working on your goals, and soon you will start to notice changes— changes in how you think, in how you see others, in how you react to situations. Things that didn't bother you before about certain movies or songs may start to prick you a little. These are the small and simple things the scriptures talk about. These are the internal improvements and adjustments that are being made little by little.

If we are constantly building the habits of the values, then, by default, we are building the strength of having the continual guidance of the Holy Ghost. We won't have to keep re-deciding what types of music to enjoy or what sites to peruse on the Internet; our doing and our being can come together in harmony as we truly live the Young Women values.

Choose *now* to serve the Lord. Choose *now* what you will do later when faced with certain situations so you aren't "carried about with every wind of doctrine" (Ephesians 4:14). Choose this moment. Write it in your journal, and remember it.

POINTS TO PONDER FROM CHAPTER 7

You may choose to ponder and pray about each concept as you answer the questions below. Plan how you can strengthen and build your testimony and act upon the principles you have studied.

How does the Lord aid us in becoming better?

Who does my Heavenly Father want me to become? How can I get there? What dos will continue helping me to be?

_____

_____

_____

_____

_____

_____

_____

_____

What is my action plan for becoming the daughter of God He and I hope for?

_____

_____

_____

_____

_____

_____

_____

_____

For further insight on making lasting change in your life, study Joshua 24:15; James 1:6; Ephesians 4:14; Alma 5; 3 Nephi 11:14; and Helaman 5:12. See also:
- Lynn G. Robbins, "What Manner of Men and Women Ought Ye to Be?" *Ensign*, May 2011;
- Kim Gibbs, *A Mighty Change of Heart* (American Fork, UT: Covenant Communications, 2013), CD.

Chapter 8

FAITH

"And now as I said concerning faith—faith is not to have a perfect knowledge of things; therefore if ye have faith ye hope for things which are not seen, which are true." (Alma 32:21)

*F*AITH IS AN action word. I'm sure you're familiar with the Primary song "Faith." I'll start you out with the first line: "Faith is knowing the sun will rise, lighting each new day."[1]

When I sang those lines in Primary, sometimes I thought, "Well, duh. Of course the sun will rise. That's how it always works." But wait—how do you know it will work tomorrow? You haven't seen it rise yet. You know it rose yesterday. You know it rose today. But you don't *know* it will rise tomorrow; you have *faith* it will rise. And yet, do you say, "Well, I'll come to your house *if* the sun rises?" or "I'll do my homework for tomorrow *if* the sun rises?" or "I'll study for the test *if* the sun rises?" No. You do things *today* to prepare for *tomorrow*, even though you haven't seen tomorrow. Do you sit on pins and needles each night, hoping that the sun will come up? No. You *expect* it. You plan for it. *That* is how you utilize faith. You do all that is required of you (finish homework, study for the test, get your dress ready for prom), and then you let go and let God do His part—a part over which you have absolutely no control. You can't make the sun rise. You must exercise your faith and prepare for when it happens.

One of my favorite stories to illustrate the perfect balance of work and belief is the story of the brother of Jared. The Jaredites were at the edge of the land and needed to cross the ocean. The Lord commanded them to build some barges and gave them direct instructions about how to do it. The Lord commanded; the brother of Jared obeyed (Ether 2:16). The brother of Jared had some concerns: in the ships, there was no light, no fresh air, and no way to steer. He went to the Lord with his questions (Ether 2:19).

There are three levels of faith in this story. First, the Lord completely took it upon Himself to solve the problem of not being able to steer. He told the brother of Jared that He would steer the ships for them, blowing the winds in the direction of the promised land. The only thing the brother of Jared had to do was enter the barges and place his full trust and faith in the promise that the Lord would indeed blow the winds for them. He believed, and the Lord delivered him from this issue (Ether 2:24). Though the scriptures don't specify, I'm pretty sure he didn't say to the Lord, "Well, you show me first. Make the winds blow, and then I'll believe you and get in the barges knowing that you will steer us to the right place." Just as we have faith that the sun will rise in the morning, he had faith that the Lord would make the winds blow.

Second, the Lord came with a direct answer to the air problem but required some work on the part of the people. He told them to drill a hole in the top and bottom of the barges and put stops in them. He then said that when they needed air, they should simply open one of the holes and let fresh air in. The brother of Jared asked questions in faith; the Lord answered (Ether 2:20).

On the question of the light, however, the Lord reversed the question and asked the brother of Jared what *he* would have the Lord do. Notice the wording in His question (He asks it twice, once in verse 23 and again in 25): "What will ye that I should do?" This, to me, represents a third level of faith: a perfect partnership with God to solve the problem.

The brother of Jared went to work. He did all that he could. There was no manual, no book, no hint of what God could, or would, do. The brother of Jared formulated a plan, and then he went into *action*. He did all he could possibly do. He knew at the onset of his plan that there would be a point at which his work would be worthless without the power of God. Yet he went to work anyway. The Lord didn't direct him; rather, the brother of Jared approached God, told Him of his solution, and then asked for help with the issues he couldn't resolve alone.

What was the result of the brother of Jared's work? (Hint: it's in Ether 3.) Man, was it work! He melted stones out of a rock. Ether 3:1 tells us they were white and clear. He then carried them to the top of the mountain. He approached the Lord in humility: "Do not be angry with thy servant because of his weakness before thee; . . . we know that thou art holy . . . and that we are unworthy before thee" (Ether 3:2). Then came the faith-filled request: "I know . . . that thou hast all power, and can do whatsoever thou wilt for the benefit of man; therefore touch these stones, O Lord, with thy finger, and prepare them that they may shine forth in darkness" (Ether 3:4).

What faith he had! Do you think you could do that? Ask the Lord to do something you had never heard of Him doing before? Have you ever come up with a plan that required much work on your part and yet was absolutely dependent upon a miracle from God to come to fruition?

Notice that in this story, the brother of Jared didn't submit the plan for preapproval. He didn't make sure the Lord would come to his aid before he went to work. (Of course, it's important also to note that he was living his life in harmony with God's will, so he would naturally formulate a plan that was within the will of God as well). Nor did he ask God to just make the wood inside the ship glow. (Wouldn't that be just as much of a miracle as God touching stones to make them shine?) No, he went to work. And he worked hard.

Yet, he came to a point where he physically could not make the plan work without the hand of the Lord (literally!). You know how it ends: Christ "touched the stones one by one with his finger" (Ether 3:6). Yes, my friends, *faith* is an action word.

I'm sure you've also read the famous scripture about faith in Alma 32, where the prophet Alma asks us to "experiment upon [his] words" (verse 27). He compares the word to a seed that will begin to grow if we find a place for it in our hearts. We will begin to understand, and it will be delicious to us. He goes on to tell us when it starts to grow, and as we continue to nourish the seed, it can become a strong tree (see verses 28–43).

That is a great metaphor and great counsel. What I like best about it, however, is not the result (although I do love tasting the deliciousness of the gospel fruit). I cherish his counsel at the very beginning, in verse 27. He talks about how we can begin to exercise faith, even to plant the seed. We don't have to have full faith yet. He says that we can exercise a "particle of faith." Our faith doesn't have to be 100 percent for us to try the experiment. More than that, he goes on to say, "even if ye can no more than *desire to believe*, let this desire work in you, even until ye believe in a manner that ye can give place for a *portion* of my words" (Alma 32:27; emphasis added).

In other words, Alma is saying, "Even if you don't think you have faith right now but *want* to have faith, start there." I call this the Wanna Wanna Principle, and I have used it many times in my own life. Sometimes, when I don't "wanna" do something, I *wish* I would want to do it; in other words, I wanna wanna do it.

For example, when I was on my mission, I had several days when I didn't want to just spring out of bed right at 6:00 a.m. to run around and shout the good tidings of the gospel, only to have people slam doors and make up excuses for not wanting to listen. (Hard to believe, I know!) On those mornings when I didn't want to go knocking, I could take that problem to the Lord and say, "Right now, I really *don't* want to go . . . but I wanna wanna go." Guess what—He took it. He took my desire to want to do the difficult parts of being a missionary (my desire to believe, as Alma calls it) and worked from there. As the morning studies progressed, I could feel my desire renewed. Sometimes it came through a verse in my scripture reading; other times it came through a conversation during companionship study. The method isn't so important as the fact that He is always there to help if we turn to Him. On the days I did this, before I knew it, I was heading out the door, actually smiling and wanting to share the good news of the gospel once again.

Many of you who are in Young Women have the opportunity to attend seminary as one of your regular classes during school hours. Many more of you have the joyous experience of attending early morning seminary. When that alarm rings in the wee hours of the morning, you may not have the greatest desire to leap out of bed and bound into your seminary class full of energy, ready to soak in every last word from your teacher. But you *do* have a desire to attend seminary and grow in the gospel. This desire is what you can take to the Lord. You can let Him help your desire to attend seminary override your desire to get sucked back into your soft, warm bed. Try it out. He will be there to grow your wanna wanna seed into a true tree.

Two truths I have learned about God are:

1. It doesn't do any good to lie to Him. He knows our desires before we even kneel down to tell Him. Christ taught that Heavenly Father knows our needs, even before we ask (3 Nephi 13:8). In other words, when we pray, we aren't giving Him any new information. When we pray, we are aligning our will to His and coming to the true desire of our hearts (Bible Dictionary: "Prayer"). C. S. Lewis gave a similar example about prayer: "It doesn't change God. It changes me."[2]

2. He will take us wherever we are in our personal journey and work with the weaknesses we turn over to Him after all we can do ourselves. And He will make it better—if we will let Him. In other words, if all we can lay on the altar at this time is a desire to have faith, He will take it. He will take it and grow it into a huge, solid tree—if we will let Him in. This is an example of the strengthening power of the Atonement.

It's okay if you don't wanna right now. Even if you wanna wanna, that's good enough to start.

Of course, the essence of faith is to have faith *in Christ*. The first principle of the gospel is faith in the Lord Jesus Christ. This is the base, the beginning. The faith that can move mountains (or light rocks for a transatlantic boat ride) is not "faith in general but . . . faith in the Lord Jesus Christ," according to Elder Russell M. Nelson.[3] This is where you build your anchor.

Faith in the latest fashion, the hottest celebrity, or even the latest and greatest scientific discovery will only lead you to a dead end. Elder Nelson goes on to explain that "*religion* literally means . . . 'to tie back' to God."[4] He then warns us of the dire consequences that can happen if we are tied to something (*anything*) other than God and Jesus Christ. When the pressure is on, where does your tie lead? Even faith in only yourself or in the ideas of man will lead to dead ends. I have always loved the visual of the warning that God gives us if we try to turn away from Him and put our faith in man: "As well might man stretch forth his puny arm to stop the Missouri river in its decreed course, or to turn it up stream, as to hinder the Almighty" (D&C 121:33). I laughed right out loud when I read that the first time. The thought of trying to turn the course of a rolling river simply by sticking in my "puny arm" somehow really brought me face to face with the knowledge of how truly, undeniably small and incapable we are on our own. Yet with faith in the Lord, the Red Sea itself can be parted (Exodus 14:14, 16, 21).

This counsel is not new. Helaman admonished his sons Nephi and Lehi to build their foundations "upon the rock of our Redeemer." What I find interesting in this counsel is what he said next: "That when the devil shall send forth his mighty winds, yea, his shafts in the whirlwind, yea, when all his hail and his mighty storm shall beat upon you, it shall have no power over you to drag you down" (Helaman 5:12). Notice he said *when* the hail comes, not *if* it comes.

Make no mistake, you are marked. You are right in the cross-hairs of Satan, and he will send forth his winds, his storms, and even his hail. He will work on you now. Why? Because if he can get you now, before you have made those eternally saving covenants in the temple, then his job is so much easier than trying to break those covenants after the fact. He will work, and he will work hard.

Don't let Satan in! Build your faith on the rock of the Savior. The rest of the verse is so comforting to me. It lets us know the protection we will be given if we do have our foundation of faith in Christ: "[Satan] shall have *no power* over you to drag you down to the gulf of misery and endless wo, because of the rock upon which ye are built, . . . a sure foundation . . . whereon if men [or women] build, they *cannot* fall" (Helaman 5:12; emphasis added). Those are some powerful promises. If you build on the rock of Christ, Satan will have "no power over you"! And we don't just have a good chance of making it, but we *cannot fall* (provided we repent when we turn ourselves away). That is incredibly encouraging.

Some of you are reading this and thinking, "But I fail—a lot—even though I build my faith on the rock." We need to look with an eternal perspective. There will be earthly falls. In fact, President Uchtdorf explained that as we set goals in an earthly sphere, we will oftentimes fail in the short run.[5] When you feel like you have fallen or failed, please remember it is temporary. In the eternally important matters, as long as we are grounded on the rock of the Redeemer and utilize repentance when needed, then just as Helaman promised, we *cannot* fail.

Faith in Christ also means faith in *His* plan for us, even when we don't fully understand that plan. Have you ever had a time where you approached God in prayer and *said* you wanted to do His will, but what you really *meant* was that you simply wanted His approval on your plan for yourself? I have. At times, we may find ourselves in the middle of situations where we truly have no idea what the purpose is. We pray to get out of it. We even sometimes provide God with the perfect pathway He can use to help us out of it. Other times we want into a certain situation—the right relationship, a good friendship, or any number of righteous desires. We even feel like we know just what the perfect relationship is that we should have and pray for that certain path. Yet our answer doesn't always seem to come (at least not in the way we asked).

Elder Neal A. Maxwell taught, "Faith in God includes faith in His purposes as well as in His timing. We cannot fully accept Him while rejecting His schedule. We cannot worship Him but insist on our plans."[6] The children of Israel experienced this when fiery serpents were among them. They asked Moses to pray that the fiery serpents would be taken away. The Lord did answer their prayers, but not in the way they expected. They were told to simply look. (Numbers 21:7–8) This seems easy enough, right? In reading this story, it seems almost crazy that anyone wouldn't look. And yet, in the Book of Mormon, Nephi tells us that many hardened their hearts, thinking it was too simple a task (and perhaps some even thought it wasn't the answer for which they had asked). They wouldn't look, and they perished (1 Nephi 17:41–42).

God sees the end from the beginning. We only see the second act of life's grand play. If you want to know what this looks like, take a picture and rip out the middle section. The middle is all we see as mortals behind the veil. God sees the whole thing, and He is the One who knows how it all connects. So often we as mortals wade through the muck in the middle with our limited perspective, and therefore it becomes even more important to place our faith in *His* view for us—an omnipotent, complete picture.

No talk of faith would be complete without mentioning the "trial of [our] faith" (1 Peter 1:7; Ether 12:6), for the trials will certainly come. President Ezra Taft Benson once said, "Every [person] eventually is backed up to the wall of faith, and there . . . must make his [or her] stand."[7] Elder Neil L. Andersen recently added, "Don't be surprised when it happens to you!"[8]

Elder Andersen warned us that leaving the shelter of the gospel due to a trial of our faith is like leaving the storm shelter in the middle of the tornado.[9] President Dieter F. Uchtdorf wisely counseled us to doubt our doubts before we doubt our faith.[10]

No one is exempt from trials of faith; God Himself tells us that we will be tried "even as Abraham" (D&C 101:4). That was some trial! Here is a father who was promised to have offspring.

In fact, he was promised to have innumerable children, to be a father of nations (see Genesis 17:1–7). That's a *lot*. Yet year after year, his wife Sarah remained barren. Does that sound like a trial of faith? Absolutely. Did Abraham doubt in God? No. His faith never wavered. When Sarah was well beyond childbearing years, she did indeed have a child (Genesis 21:2–3). So we see that with God, all things are possible. But the trial of Abraham's faith was not over.

When his son Isaac was still young, Abraham was commanded to sacrifice him to God (Genesis 22:1–10). As a parent, I cannot even begin to comprehend what this must have felt like to Abraham. To go against every parental instinct to protect your beloved child from harm in order to obey God seems to me an excruciating trial of faith. It was an incredible trial, but he was willing to do it (Genesis 22:11–14).

Do you think God knew what Abraham would do? I think He did. God knew Abraham's heart. However, as Elder Hugh B. Brown explained about his trial, perhaps "Abraham needed to learn something about Abraham."[11]

Likewise, God counsels us to look to Him in all things, to "doubt not, fear not" (D&C 6:36). One of the first things Christ taught to the Nephites when He came to visit them after His Resurrection was to not be "of little faith" (3 Nephi 13:30).

Yes, faith is knowing the sun will rise, and doing everything we can (through thick and thin) to be ready when it does.

POINTS TO PONDER FROM CHAPTER 8

You may choose to ponder and pray about each concept as you answer the questions below. Plan how you can strengthen and build your testimony and act upon the principles you have studied.

What does it mean to have faith in the Savior Jesus Christ?

_____
_____
_____
_____
_____
_____
_____

Did it matter what the brother of Jared chose to provide for light in the boats? Might the Lord have accepted any thoughtful solution?

_____
_____
_____
_____
_____
_____
_____

How can I develop a deeper faith in the Savior? What is my action plan to strengthen my faith?

_____
_____
_____
_____
_____
_____
_____

WE ARE DAUGHTERS OF OUR HEAVENLY FATHER

When have I exhibited faith?

_____
_____
_____
_____
_____
_____
_____
_____
_____

For further insight on faith, study Alma 32; Ether 12:6–22; 1 Corinthians 10:13; Psalm 46:10; and D&C 101:16. See also:

- Jean A. Stevens, "'Fear Not; I Am with Thee,'" *Ensign*, May 2014;
- Russell M. Nelson, "Let Your Faith Show," *Ensign*, May 2014;
- Dieter F. Uchtdorf, "The Best Time to Plant a Tree," *Ensign*, January 2014;
- Neal A. Maxwell, *That Ye May Believe* (Salt Lake City: Bookcraft, 1992);
- Ezra Taft Benson, "The Book of Mormon Is the Word of God," *Ensign*, January 1988;
- Neil L. Andersen, "Trial of Your Faith," *Ensign*, November 2012;
- Jeffrey R. Holland, "Cast Not Away Therefore Your Confidence," *BYU Speeches*, 2 March 1999;
- Dieter F. Uchtdorf, "Come, Join with Us," *Ensign*, November 2013.

Chapter 9

DIVINE NATURE

"Be partakers of the divine nature. . . . Giving all diligence, add to your faith virtue; and to virtue knowledge; and to knowledge temperance; and to temperance patience; and to patience godliness; and to godliness brotherly kindness; and to brotherly kindness charity." (2 Peter 1:4–7)

YOU ARE THE daughter of a Father. You are the daughter of a King. You are the daughter of a God.

I remember in 2011 watching the wedding of a prince and a princess-to-be—Prince William and Kate Middleton. It was a fairy tale come true, and the world watched in awe. While witnessing all of the pomp and circumstance that went into the wedding, my mind couldn't help but wander to our own divinity. I wanted to jump through the TV screen and tell every small girl who was watching, wearing her own little plastic tiara and dress-up gown, "*You are* a princess! You are so much more than the world would have you think. This role is not reserved for the few, the lucky, the 'chosen.' *You are chosen*. You have been chosen from before the world began. *You* are of royal birth by the most royal of all fathers. And He wants you to come home. At the end of the day, He wants you back in His kingdom, to rule and reign with Him for *eternity*."

I want you to stop and really think about this for a moment. Let it sink in. The most you have here on this earth is a good 116 years (or 123, if Bolivian records are correct).[1] So, on a good-luck spree, you've got 100 years here. Seems like a long time, right? A lifetime! Do something for me. Get a skein of yarn. String the whole thing out. Yep, the whole thing. Keep going. Get it all. Don't worry; I'll wait. Now go get a toothpick. Pick any random spot on that line and lay the toothpick at a 90-degree angle over the yarn. *That intersection* is your life here compared to your eternal existence.

Really.

When you get back to heaven, earth life will be a blink. When you get there, you will realize that you *are* a princess. Your Father is waiting to empower you with all the riches of the *universe*. More than that, He is waiting to help you reach your true potential, a goddess of the Most High.

Let's say that you were to marry the Prince of England. How would you act? How would you dress? Knowing that you represent a nation, how would you conduct yourself? What would your speech sound like?

You represent all of heaven with how you act, how you conduct yourself, and how you speak. Does any of your outward behavior need to change to be true to the divinity inside of you?

Yes, you are that princess, just maybe not in the worldly sense. But in the end, does that really matter? God is there. Your Father in Heaven is there. Never forget that. No matter your circumstances here on earth, no matter how small and worthless you feel, *never* forget that you are of *royal* heritage.

Okay, so you've heard this talk before about everything that waits for you *after* life, but what about now? How do you get through those horrible days when friends turn into enemies? When someone's words become daggers thrown into your back? When it seems like everywhere you turn, people are bent on tearing you down?

Those are the times that you need to remember this most of all: *God never forgets you.* He has promised that He won't leave you, nor will He forget you. Nor will your Lord and Savior, Jesus Christ, forget you. He has "graven thee upon the palms of [His] hands" (Isaiah 49:16; 1 Nephi 21:16). He will not forget you. You are His sister. You are God's daughter.

You are divine. The beauty of this is that you didn't (and don't) have to *do* anything to earn divinity; it is *in* you. It's not something you earn. It's something you *are*. Don't be fooled by Satan's tactic of making you feel like nothing. He may be there in your mind, constantly telling you that you are worthless, and his voice becomes even louder with every mistake you make. Anytime you veer from the path, he is suddenly right there telling you that God wouldn't want you now, that now you have blown it.

Stop.

Don't listen to that message.

Instead, let yourself be calm and quiet. Go somewhere. Shut out the voices. Shut off the media. Take out the earphones. Unplug. Let the silence in, and just listen. Let that still small voice in (see 1 Kings 19:12; 1 Nephi 17:45). It's there. If you let go of the hate and the hurt, it's there: the quiet but steady voice. It's telling you that you are His daughter. You are a child of royal birth. You are a chosen vessel. And you don't—no, you *can't*— *do* anything to earn this. It is inherent as part of your divine lineage.

Your divinity is your birthright. Don't sell it for a mess of pottage (Genesis 25:29–34). Live up to it. Listen to it. Cling to it. Believe it. And *live* it.

Now, please don't misunderstand; there are many examples where prophets have called to our attention our own carnal state of nothingness when compared to God (see Mosiah 4:5; Alma 26:12; Helaman 12:7). This simply means that without God, we truly are nothing. It is only in partnering with the power of God that we can reach our true divine potential.

It almost seems like a great paradox—next to God, man is nothing, yet "the worth of souls is great in the sight of God" (D&C 18:10). President Uchtdorf summed this up beautifully: "This is a paradox of man: compared to God, man is nothing; yet we are everything to God."[2] Yes, we know that in this phase of our eternal existence, we truly are nothing. Yet as President Uchtdorf goes on to explain, "We have a spark of eternal fire burning within our breast. We have the incomprehensible promise of exaltation—worlds without end—within our grasp. And it is God's great desire to help us reach it."[3] That phenomenon is both humbling and inspiring to me.

How do we rise to the divinity within us? Here is where the beauty comes in—the beauty of the Atonement. Through the grace of the Atonement, you can truly claim that divinity within you. Some of you about now may say that you may have had that divine potential when you were born, but that was a long time ago. You may think you have gone too far, have done too much to ever be able to become whole again and truly be the divine daughter you were born to be. God promises that through Christ's Atonement scarlet can be made white as snow, crimson red can be as wool (Isaiah 1:18). That's pretty drastic.

Still don't believe me? Still believe that you are too far gone? Let's look at Paul, from the New Testament, the great Apostle of Christ. He traveled to many places and preached the doctrines of Christ. He was mocked and suffered greatly, but he never wavered in his testimony of Christ and eventually was even martyred for his belief in Christ. If you don't know of him, you have most likely still read his words—Romans, 1 and 2 Corinthians, Galatians, Ephesians, Philippians, Colossians, 1 and 2 Thessalonians, 1 and 2 Timothy, Titus, Philemon, and Hebrews.

But here's what you may not know so well: before Paul was Paul the great Apostle, he was Saul the great persecutor. Yep, they're the very same. He was heavily involved in the persecution of the early Saints. He was even part of stoning the Apostle Stephen. I think it's safe to say that he was one of the bad guys in the biblical plot. One day, while he was on his way to cause more trouble in Damascus—namely to arrest some of the Church leaders—Christ appeared personally to ask Saul why he was persecuting Him (Acts 9:4–5).

I won't go into great details of the rest of the story (it's in Acts 9—a great read), but here's the condensed version: Saul was struck down and blinded. Christ then approached Ananias, one of the Church leaders in Damascus (most likely one of the people on Saul's list to arrest), and told him that Saul needed his help. Can you just picture that exchange?

"Ananias, I want you to go help Saul."

"Saul? Did I hear that name right? As in the bad guy who is after me?"

"Yes. That's the one."

Okay, so it isn't scripted exactly like that, but that's about how it goes down. The key is in Acts 9:15, after Ananias had just told Christ that Saul was not a very good man. Christ's response was, "Go . . . for he is a chosen vessel unto me."

Whoa. Christ had just called the bad guy a "chosen vessel." And Saul had not done *one* thing to earn it. Christ knew the potential within Saul even before *Saul* was aware of it. Christ knew his nature—his *divine* nature.

President Uchtdorf put this eloquently when he stated, "The Lord uses a scale very different from the world's to weigh the worth of a soul."[4] Yes, God truly knows us, even better than we know ourselves. He understands our divinity, and He foresees our potential to reach that divinity.

If you were to ask most parents who have held their own newborn baby for a few moments, they'd say they would gladly give their life for their precious little one. The love is complete. It is all encompassing. But wait—what has the baby done for the parent? Nothing. The baby's infinite worth exists on its own. Just by *being*, the baby is divine. For the mother and father, their child is literally a piece of them. You are a piece of God. You have that divinity in you simply by existing.

You are a child of a Father who is heavenly. You have the potential, the nature to be heavenly too. In 1989, President Gordon B. Hinckley challenged God's daughters everywhere to "rise to the stature of the divine within you."[5] What are you going to do to live up to your true divine nature?

POINTS TO PONDER FROM CHAPTER 9

You may choose to ponder and pray about each concept as you answer the questions below. Plan how you can strengthen and build your testimony and act upon the principles you have studied.

Do I accept that I have a divine nature? Why or why not?

_____

_____

_____

_____

_____

_____

_____

_____

How do we betray our divine nature (or sell it for a mess of pottage)?

_____

_____

_____

_____

_____

_____

_____

_____

How can I "rise to the stature of the divine within [me]," living and reaching my potential as a daughter of God?

_____

_____

_____

_____

_____

_____

_____

_____

How does my treatment of others reflect what I know about the individual worth and divine nature of men and women?

_____

_____

_____

_____

_____

_____

_____

How can I help others recognize their own divine nature, especially those who struggle with self-worth?

_____

_____

_____

_____

_____

_____

_____

How can my understanding of this value help me through my trials?

_____

_____

_____

_____

_____

_____

_____

For more insight on your divine nature, study Moses 1:1–26.
See also:
- Dieter F. Uchtdorf, "You Matter to Him," *Ensign*, November 2011;
- Gordon B. Hinckley, "Rise to the Stature of the Divine within You," *Ensign*, November 1989.

Chapter 10

INDIVIDUAL WORTH

"Remember the worth of souls is great in the sight of God."
(D&C 18:10)

AVE YOU EVER wondered why both divine nature and individual worth are in the Young Women theme? Don't they both mean about the same thing? Let me try to give a distinction. I recently gave birth to my seventh child. I love all of my children—they are my offspring. They all have a part of me in them. Yet, they are each very much their own person. They are each individually unique in their thoughts, gifts, and talents. Does it mean I love any one of them more? Not in the least. I love them each individually, on their own. Even my twins, who shared every pre-birth minute together, are incredibly individual. And each has incalculable worth to me. Their worth is equal, but it's also individual.

Let's look at some other examples. We know from reading the Book of Mormon that Lehi had at least six sons. Some were righteous, and others were . . . not so righteous (1 Nephi). I used to read the first pages of the Book of Mormon and get so upset with Lehi. After all, Laman and Lemuel caused problems for the entire crew from day one. They complained, mocked, and even tried to kill their siblings. They were constantly whining about going back to Jerusalem, where they could continue to live the good life they had known and loved from their youth.

Years ago as I read these parts, I thought to Lehi, "Good grief. Just let them go back already! I've read ahead, and they do nothing but cause problems the entire rest of their lives, and then they cause many generations of people to be led astray after their crazy ideas" (see Mosiah 10:11–17). Yet it seems every chance he got, Lehi was continually teaching, working with, and even pleading with them to choose the right: "He did exhort them then with all the feeling of a tender parent" (1 Nephi 8:37) to choose the right and taste of the greatness of God.

Now, after becoming a parent, I can imagine how Lehi must have felt, having seen a vision in which two of his sons would not come and partake of the greatest gift imaginable, even the gift of eternal life, and feel the love of God (1 Nephi 8:12, 18). After gaining a pretty good idea that his sons were perhaps not going to make it back to the celestial kingdom, did he cut them off and walk away? No. Not in the least bit. He never gave up on them. They were worth too much to Lehi for him to ever give up on them.

I didn't learn the inexplicable love of a parent until I became one myself—and that love just keeps enlarging! Their worth does not diminish by the experiences they have or the choices they make in life. I have known many parents throughout my life who have had children veer from the path of the gospel. In every case, not once did I ever hear the parents denounce their love for their child, nor their child's worth. I have seen parents question, plead, and cry over their lost children. It is heartrending to watch. Their love for these precious souls never diminishes.

I cannot even begin to comprehend the love that God and Jesus Christ have for each one of us personally. I know that we hear all the time, "Even if I were the only person on earth, Christ still would have gone through the Atonement for me." This is hard for me to grasp, and even harder to explain, but let me try to give an example that is utterly incomparable to the vast greatness of the

Atonement but does help me gain a tiny bit of insight of the love He felt for each individual during His eternal atoning sacrifice.

When my twins were born, they were 100 percent dependent on me for their lives. I fed them, dressed them, held them, and cared for them in every way. Without me performing these acts of love, oftentimes around the clock, they would not have survived past the first few days of being in my home. If I had only had a single child, would I have said to myself, "Since there is only one, I don't need to do any of those things; only if I had several would it be worth the effort"? That seems a bit crazy. Even now, with more children, I continue to make meals for them, even spoon-feeding the younger ones, which helps them survive from day to day. If I only had one child, would I be prone to not make meals because I wasn't doing so for multiple kids? Of course not—even the thought is preposterous.

I wonder if this is how Christ views our questioning of His atoning sacrifice as a personal, saving act. He did it just as much for each one of us individually as He did for all of us collectively.

The act of saving souls is done on an individual basis. When you go to the temple to do baptisms for the dead, you do one baptism for each person. Think about that. Billions of people have died and are waiting to receive these eternal ordinances, so why don't we just read a big list of names and then get baptized once to cover everyone at the same time? God is so intent on saving "the one" that each and every person receives these ordinances for him or herself. The same is also true of the other ordinances of the temple; each is performed on an individual basis.

We are all divine offspring of God. He loves us collectively as His children. But He also loves each one of us individually as His son or daughter.

Let's go back to the phrase *individual worth*. Let's break it apart just for a bit. Think of the word *individual*. You are unique. You are completely you. Not one person who has lived or will live thinks, experiences, or chooses his or her course in exactly the same way you will. I feel like sometimes we get the notion that we are all supposed to conform to be exactly the same in the Church, but it is actually quite the opposite. We need every kind of talent and ability, working together in unison to move the kingdom of God forward. Just as Heavenly Father, Jesus Christ, and the Holy Ghost are different and distinct Personages but are one in purpose, so also should we strive to be in the gospel—one in purpose but also realizing, and even relishing, our own different and unique talents and gifts that we can use to further God's work on the earth. In fact, He tells us that He purposefully gave us all different gifts (see D&C 46:10–26; 1 Corinthians 12:1–11). He specifically says that no one has every gift, but everyone has at least one gift (D&C 46:11). He also warns us not to let those unique gifts come between us; they are not things by which to compare ourselves to others, but rather, they are gifts to be used in unity—just as all of the different body parts are used to contribute to the complete function of the human body.

Paul explains perfectly the problem that can come from devaluing our own individuality, as well as diminishing the individuality of others. In 1 Corinthians 12:16–17, he warns, "And if the ear shall say, Because I am not the eye, I am not of the body; is it therefore not of the body? If the whole body were an eye, where were the hearing? If the whole were hearing, where were the smelling?" This analogy brings it to such a simple level. We could easily put our own feelings into those phrases. If I have not been given the gift of singing, am I not important in the Church? After all, we know how important music is in the gospel. But if everyone could only sing, who would give the great youth conference talks? If everyone could only speak, who would play the piano for the great musical numbers? If everyone gave talks all the time, who would be there to listen and feel the Spirit? What about great girls' camp planners or nursery leaders? Secretaries, teachers, den leaders? The list could go on. There is a use for every single one of you, with each of your unique talents and contributions.

We are each so individual and different—so different, in fact, that we may take it to the extreme and think we don't really fit into the "gospel mold." Sure, if you take an eye and a foot and place them next to each other, they may feel like they are less than compatible. But the beauty comes when we can see the whole picture, when we can see the picture that God sees: how important our individuality is to the whole of the body of Christ—His entire flock of Saints in the gospel.

That is all great in theory. Yes, we as individuals have merit in the gospel. But let's face it—at times many of us question our individual *worth*. It is so easy to lose track of the eternal aspect of our worth when all around us the world is screaming about our changing worth, or sometimes our lack of worth.

I would like you to picture in your mind a nice, crisp, clean $100 bill. That's worth quite a bit, wouldn't you agree? Would you like to have it? I know I would! Now imagine that I take that clean, crisp $100 bill and crumple it up in my hand. And I do it over and over again until it has permanent wrinkles and crumples. No matter what I do, it is never going to be that crisp, clean, brand-new bill again. Now how much is it worth? What? It's worth $100 still? Why? It's not new. It's not fresh. Why is it worth exactly the same as it was from the moment it came off the printing press? Why didn't its value diminish when I mishandled it? Now imagine that I take the same not-so-new-but-still-worth-$100 bill, put it on the ground, and stomp on it. Repeatedly. Let's say that it gets thrown in the mud and run over by a car. Let's say that it even gets some tears and rips in it. *Now* how much is it worth? It's still worth $100? But it's not new. It's not pretty. It's not even clean! If you smelled it, it would even stink a little bit. It's not wearing the right clothes or the right shoes. It doesn't always say the hippest things. It may not even be that "smart." If I were to offer this bill to you—this tattered, torn, wrinkly, dirty $100 bill—would you take it? Why?

Because nothing that happens on the outside of this bill can take away its inherent value, its *worth*.

You are worth *so much more* than you may give yourself credit for. There is nothing that can happen *to* you that can take away the worth *within* you. You are an individual to God—an individual, *not* just one of the masses—and you have *worth*, just like a bill but *priceless*. Your Heavenly Father's whole purpose is to bring about your immortality and your eternal life. You are worth every drop of blood that Christ spilled in Gethsemane.

You. Are. Worth it.

Do you want proof that He knows you personally? Read 3 Nephi 11:15. This is the key to the whole Book of Mormon, the climax about which every prophet had previously testified—that Christ would come to the Americas. We read in 3 Nephi 11 that Christ came and testified that He was Jesus Christ. And then He had the entire population come up *one by one*. It wasn't just a "Here I am; you can see that I am real" event. He had them come individually (3 Nephi 11:14–15). He knew each one by name. He knows *you* by name. He knows your worth. And it is so much more than what the world would have you believe. Don't buy into Satan's lie that you're not enough.

Stop making comparisons. Stop feeling guilt for not measuring up to the world's idea of what worth is or is not. Stop trying to fit into a world that is going downhill fast. Stand up. Stand strong. Stand out. Your worth is enough to the Lord—just by you being yourself.

POINTS TO PONDER FROM CHAPTER 10

You may choose to ponder and pray about each concept as you answer the questions below. Plan how you can strengthen and build your testimony and act upon the principles you have studied.

Study D&C 18:10–16.

WE ARE DAUGHTERS OF OUR HEAVENLY FATHER

Why did the Savior suffer the Atonement for me? Who am I to God? Why am I worth so much to Heavenly Father and Jesus Christ? Will anything change my worth to God?

_____
_____
_____
_____
_____
_____
_____

Do I believe and accept that I have individual worth? How can I increase my testimony of my individual worth?

_____
_____
_____
_____
_____
_____
_____

What things or people cause me to question my individual worth? How will I combat the thoughts and messages from Satan that cause me to doubt my worth and my potential?

_____
_____
_____
_____
_____
_____
_____

For further insight on your individual worth, study Moses 1:1–26. See also:

- Russell M. Nelson, "Woman—Of Infinite Worth," *Ensign*, November 1989;
- Elaine L. Jack, "Identity of a Young Woman," *Ensign*, November 1989.

Chapter 11

KNOWLEDGE

"Seek learning, even by study and also by faith." (D&C 88:118)

YOU WILL NEVER use your knowledge as much as within the walls of your own home, teaching your children and enhancing your own life and mission on the earth. President Hinckley once recounted a story of Brigham Young, who was asked what he would do if he had to choose between educating his sons or his daughters. He said that he would educate his daughters, because they would be the mothers of his grandchildren.[1] How true that is! You will do so much educating at home; it is vital that you gain all of the knowledge that you can.

God Himself states outright: "Whatever principle of intelligence we attain unto in this life, it will rise with us in the resurrection" (D&C 130:18). Although you will eventually finish school, your learning will never cease. We are counseled to constantly grow and learn. In fact, in the same section of Doctrine and Covenants, God goes on to tell us that "if a person gains more knowledge and intelligence in this life . . . he will have so much the advantage in the world to come" (verse 19).

Knowledge is so important that God has also given us the following counsel: "Seek ye out of the best books words of wisdom, seek learning even by study and also by faith" (D&C 109:7). Yes,

I think it's safe to assume that learning and growing in knowledge is of utmost importance to Heavenly Father.

The Bible Dictionary states that knowledge is one of the attributes of God and "knowledge of divine and spiritual things is absolutely essential for one's salvation" (Bible Dictionary, "Knowledge"). It is an *essential* ingredient for salvation. In other words, we can't get there through faith alone. Look up James 2:17 and remember that we need to put our faith into action, putting forth our own efforts to grow in knowledge.

I really like what comes next in the Bible Dictionary. We are not expected to know all things at once. We are told that we learn things "precept upon precept; line upon line; . . . here a little, and there a little" (Isaiah 28:10). I love that concept. The Lord doesn't expect us to master calculus on our first day of first grade. In fact, just before that scripture, Isaiah says that we teach knowledge to "them that are weaned from the milk" (verse 9), which actually has two different meanings, according to the footnotes. One means you start learning early (footnote b). The other, as cited in the Doctrine and Covenants, denotes that some young ones cannot bear the "meat" but must first be given the "milk" (footnote c; D&C 19:22).

This concept shows the total love of God for each one of us individually, as well as the importance He places on educating every one of His children. He doesn't say our children must wait until a certain age to begin learning. In fact, if you go into any nursery in the church, you will see lessons being taught. These are eighteen-month-old toddlers! And they are being taught the basic concepts of the gospel—the "milk," if you will. Growing line upon line, we then become ready to learn at deeper levels.

The beauty of this is we don't have to skip and jump beyond our current knowledge; God loves us and accepts us where we are at any given time. Then He takes us by the hand and leads us higher—if we will let Him.[2] I don't expect my second grader to be doing the algebra problems my seventh grader is doing, nor do I expect my seventh grader to be doing the calculus problems she'll be learning in high school. I simply help my children and let them grow at their individual knowledge levels. Knowing they still have more to learn doesn't make them any less valuable to me now. I still love them both completely. I want them to grow and learn more because I see how knowledge will help open so many doors for them in life.

This is the way God views you. Never forget that your worth is not dependent upon what you do or do not know. He is helping you gain knowledge for your benefit, not His. Brad Wilcox explains this so beautifully when he points out that heaven is not something we *earn*; it is something we *learn*.[3]

Look at the methods Christ used to help people to gain knowledge while He was on the earth. Didn't He teach in the pattern of meeting us where we are? He did so much teaching in parables, permitting the people to learn the lesson at their own level and rate (see Matthew 13:9–13). This is likely one of the reasons we are counseled to read and reread the scriptures throughout our lives. Each time we ponder the same stories, we approach them with greater knowledge and can therefore understand principles in a different or extended realm than the first time we read them. Sometimes I will be reviewing the same story I have read multiple times before, and I actually have the thought, "Hey, when did they add this to the story? It wasn't there the last time I read this. It takes on a whole new meaning to me now."

So many young women have told me they feel like their goals and dreams of gaining knowledge and their goal of becoming a mother present an either/or choice. This is not the case. These two activities—gaining knowledge and raising righteous children— are not mutually exclusive but harmonious activities. No amount of knowledge, experience, or education you gain will ever be lost or wasted. Every ounce of education you receive will help to make you a better mother. Picture this: Prior to your birth, a loving Father in Heaven hugs you, one of His choice spirits. He gives you His last bit of advice and encouragement, and then He sends you to earth. Perhaps He blesses you with a worthy and righteous mother and father to teach you the lessons that will help you return to Him. You grow in life and you learn. Your knowledge increases.

Then, as you become a mother, He puts His utmost trust in you. He is counting on *you* to help bring *His* child back home to Him. I so hope you can feel the importance of your role as a mother in God's kingdom on earth. It is not a secondhand job. There is no such thing as "just a mom." Abraham Lincoln said, "All that I am, or ever hope to be, I owe to my angel mother."[4]

You are God's first and greatest hope in bringing to pass His work. Above all else, please, please never forget that there is nothing more noble or important than aiding God with the great work you will do as a mother of His spirit sons and daughters. And believe me, you need every ounce of knowledge to prepare you for this great task.

I know you have probably heard talks about all of the different jobs that are entailed in motherhood. Within a matter of hours, mothers go from being chefs to mathematicians, from taxi drivers to nurses, from judges to carpenters, from accountants to dance instructors, from cheerleaders to managers, from consultants to lawyers, from detectives to night watchmen. Mothers truly are all professions combined into one (without the benefit of sick leave or vacation days!). Do you really think choosing to get an education or learning something for your own benefit would not be helpful? To prove the point, George Washington himself said, "All I am I owe to my mother. I attribute all my success in life to the moral, intellectual, and physical education I received from her."[5]

Have you ever noticed that there is not one perfect mold of a good mother? As a mother, you don't give up your dreams. You don't give up who you are. How you find the balance is a personal and individual road. What works for one person will not work for another. On your unique road to following your dreams, you will need to decide how you will find your own balance. The principle is to continue gaining knowledge throughout your life. How you put that principle into action is up to you. The principle does not change; the commandment and responsibility to increase your knowledge will never be retracted. Knowledge is not something that will fall into your lap while you sit and surf channels at night. It is yet another way in which you must be actively pursuing a path. The path will differ for almost everyone, but we must all be pursuers of this great quest, not just passive bystanders.

Becoming a mother is not the end of your quest for knowledge. In fact, in many ways it is the beginning. The lessons you learn about motherhood during your years in Young Women are part of the plan of salvation. Learning through our families and church attendance is the Lord's designed method to help us continually progress. We have a relationship with our children like God has with us. It's a huge part of how we grow in our knowledge of certain aspects of godhood.

I find it interesting that in God's counsel to seek learning and knowledge, He never gives a precise list of what specific fields of study we should enter. As Elder Russell M. Nelson recently advised students at BYU–Hawaii, "Brothers *and sisters*, don't be afraid to pursue your goals—even your dreams! There is no shortcut to excellence and competence. Education is the difference between wishing you could help other people and being able to help them."[6] Two things struck me when I read that quote. First, he didn't just address the boys of the group; he counseled all of us to follow our dreams in our studies. The second hit me hard: our receiving an education is the difference between wishing we could help and actually being able to help. That is powerful. In the *For the Strength of Youth* pamphlet, we are further told, "Education is an investment that brings great rewards and will open the doors of opportunity that may otherwise be closed to you."[7] If you don't have a plan to actively pursue your education right now, make one. Be proactive. Hanging out for a year to "find yourself" is not a plan. It doesn't matter if you have your sights set on attending Harvard, attending the local community college, or learning a trade. The point is that you have a plan. If you think it can't be done, you have been talking to the wrong people. Even if you think your goals seem unachievable in your current family circumstances, ask your leaders or school counselors to help you find a way to make it happen.

Regardless of what awaits you in the future—mission, no mission; marriage, no marriage; kids, no kids; political office, home office—God will use *your* specific talents and gifts to help in building His kingdom on earth. And gaining knowledge is one of the greatest ways you can discover your individual strengths and talents. Knowledge is so much more than opening books and taking tests. It is personal fulfillment.

Additionally, gaining marketable skills along with a formal education will empower you to support yourself and your family should you need to do so. Illness, unemployment, divorce, death, and other family emergencies often necessitate a mother working outside of her home. Being ready and able to support your family will bring you both comfort and peace in ever-changing circumstances, especially in times of financial instability or uncertainty.

Many options exist for furthering your education. Even outside the formal graded classroom, there are often community classes you can take. The arts of singing, dancing, writing, and painting are just a few examples of the countless ways in which you may increase your knowledge throughout life. There is a whole world out there filled with learning moments. You just need to soak them in and let them become part of a new and better you. And then you share that with God's children while they are in your care.

One incredible woman I know struggled with traditional education all through school. After her first year of college, she realized that a formal college education was not what she wanted to pursue. What she did have was a passion for hair design. She got the opportunity to apprentice at an elite hair design studio and snatched it. Even now, she is one of the most gifted hair stylists I have ever known. Not only has she been able to bless the lives of her children with her talent and knowledge in this field, people from all around flock to her home to get the perfect "Gina" cut. She has been able to beautifully mold and fit her personal dreams and passion with her full-time motherhood role.

President Hinckley urged every young woman to gain as much education as she can, both for her hands and her mind. He then said to use your education to bless the society around you. He stated, "There is an essence of the divine in the improvement of the mind."[8] How beautifully poetic to talk about how important gaining intelligence is to God (see D&C 93:36).

Can we ever say we have learned enough? Absolutely not. We will be learning and growing even past the day we die. We will be learning and growing well into the eternities (and I think I am going to need well into the eternities to understand some of the deeper concepts). Brigham Young stated, "We might ask, when shall we cease to learn? I will give you my opinion about it: never, never."[9]

Even Christ Himself learned in this manner. In Luke we read that "Jesus increased in wisdom and stature, and in favour with God and man" (Luke 2:52). And this was after He had astonished the high priests in Jerusalem with His knowledge of the things of God!

In our quest for knowledge, we are not on our own—far from it. The Lord sends us help. Part of the mission of the Holy Ghost is to help "teach [us] all things" and "bring all things to [our] remembrance" (John 14:26). Boy, did I ever use that promise during my school years. And you can too. It is there, given to us when we were confirmed after our baptism: the gift of the Holy Ghost. He's there, not only to help you discern between right and wrong, but to help you progress toward His kingdom. Isn't that just beautiful? Use that gift. Let Him help you.

Further, gaining "earthly knowledge" does not need to be separated from our spiritual growth at all. God tells us that to Him all things are spiritual. When you are increasing in knowledge with your scholastic studies, you are actually increasing in your spiritual knowledge as well (D&C 29:34). Part of the mission of the Holy Ghost is to teach and help us discern truth in any situation—at home, at school, at work, at play. The Holy Ghost can help you discern the truths taught in school and during your education, especially when you are being taught lessons in an increasingly secular society.

We may think in some cases that we are learning scientific laws that have nothing to do with God. It is actually the other way around. All of the "latest and greatest" scientific discoveries are merely man's realization of laws that God already knows and follows. He uses those laws too (see D&C 88:42–61).[10]

One of my favorite—and most spiritual, believe it or not—classes was anatomy, the study of the human body. I remember so vividly sitting in that class, learning about all of the muscles, bones, tendons, joints, and nerves that comprise the human body. It was truly mind-boggling to study all of the details that enable the functioning of this physical being. I remember being overcome by the witness that God truly is at the helm of our existence and that we really are His supreme creation.

I loved that my professor was also continuing to learn through faith in God. One day when we were learning about the origin and insertion of the Achilles tendon, we were talking about how its position makes it more susceptible to injuries than other tendons in the body. Someone asked why it was positioned that way. He looked straight at the student and said, "You're going to have to take that one up with the Maker; I have no idea." What a powerful lesson his answer was for me. Though this professor knew a lot, he was still humble and submissive to the fact that he didn't have all the answers yet (see Alma 7:23). But he knew who *does* have all the answers. That was a poignant lesson to me to always turn to God at whatever stage of knowledge I may be in at the time.

Jacob issued a warning to not place too much pride in what we know: "When they are learned they think they are wise, and they hearken not unto the counsel of God, for they set it aside, supposing they know of themselves, wherefore, their wisdom is foolishness and it profiteth them not. . . . But to be learned is good if they hearken unto the counsels of God" (2 Nephi 9:28–29).

Truly, the heart of knowledge is to build on the core of the gospel. This is where the Personal Progress program can aid you in your quest to build your knowledge base for the kingdom of God. The purpose of the value goals and projects is to build your spiritual knowledge base. Of all the learning in which you engage, this is the most vital in helping structure your homes of eternal materials, impregnable to the storms of Satan. Build a deep spiritual reservoir from which you and your future family can be sustained. President Kimball counseled, "I stress again the deep need each woman has to study the scriptures. We want our homes to be blessed with sister scriptorians—whether you are single or married, young or old, widowed or living in a family."[11] Start now. Build with daily deposits, no matter how small. Through the years, those small steps in studying the scriptures will pay huge dividends as you use that wealth of knowledge to help others.

POINTS TO PONDER FROM CHAPTER 11

You may choose to ponder and pray about each concept as you answer the questions below. Plan how you can strengthen and build your testimony and act upon the principles you have studied.

Read D&C 88:77–80. Why is it important for me to increase my knowledge?

_____
_____
_____
_____
_____
_____
_____
_____

What level of education would I like to obtain? What am I interested in learning? What can I learn that will be marketable? How will I provide for my family?

_____
_____
_____
_____
_____
_____
_____

What are my talents, and how can I improve upon them?

_____
_____
_____
_____
_____
_____
_____
_____

What is God's mission for me? (Refer to your patriarchal blessing and prayer for help in discerning this.) What do I need to learn and do to accomplish my mission?

_____
_____
_____
_____
_____
_____
_____

What is my plan for being a lifelong learner?

_____
_____
_____
_____
_____
_____
_____

For further insight on gaining knowledge, study D&C 11:21. See also:

- *True to the Faith* (Salt Lake City: The Church of Jesus Christ of Latter-day Saints, 2004), 50–51;
- David A. Bednar, *Increase in Learning* (Salt Lake City: Deseret Book, 2011), especially the preface;
- *Teachings of Presidents of the Church: Brigham Young* (Salt Lake City: The Church of Jesus Christ of Latter-day Saints, 1997), 192–201;
- Gordon B. Hinckley, "Our Responsibility to Our Young Women," *Ensign*, September 1988;
- Russell M. Nelson, "Youth of the Noble Birthright: What Will You Choose?" CES Devotional, 6 September 2013;
- N. Eldon Tanner, "The Laws of God," *Ensign*, November 1975.

CHOICE
and
ACCOUNTABILITY

"Choose you this day whom ye will serve; . . . but as for me and my house, we will serve the Lord." (Joshua 24:15)

PRESIDENT MONSON TELLS us about the three Rs of choice and accountability: the right of choice, the responsibility of choice, and the results of choice (our accountability to those choices).[1]

Right of choice: We came to this world with moral agency—the ability to make choices for ourselves. In fact, this was the key to our coming to this world, that we valued agency so much. This is the path we chose. Former prophet David O. McKay taught, "Next to the bestowal of life itself, the right to direct that life is God's greatest gift to man. . . . Freedom of choice is more to be treasured than any possession earth can give."[2] The right to choose was the foundation for the entire war in heaven. Satan wanted desperately to take that right away from us.

The war has not ended; it has just changed locations. Satan hasn't changed; he still desires and works incessantly to take away our right to choose. How does he do that? He actually tries to use our choices to bind us to him, where in the end he can have total power over us (see 2 Nephi 28:8, 19–20). The irony of this goal is the fact that many of his lies try to convince us that the rules of the gospel are restrictive and binding, and he tempts us with choosing to be "free" from the rules and regulations. In the end, our freedom is the last thing on Satan's agenda; he wants us to be slaves to him, and he accomplishes that when he successfully leads us from the *safety* and *freedom* inherent in the gospel standards and the commandments of God.

Many people question the existence of God, asking why, if there really is a God, do so many bad things happen to good people? That reasoning is no good. We experience adversity for different reasons—our own actions, others' actions, or it's just part of life. But even when we face trials because of the bad choices of others, God is there, and He is watching. He values our right to agency so intensely that He will not step in to take it away, even when we are choosing things that will not bring us back home to Him (see 2 Nephi 2:27). In no way, however, does this mean He doesn't care.

When God showed to one of the great prophets, Enoch, a vision of things to come, He wept when they reviewed the people of Noah's time (Moses 7:28). Enoch was incredibly surprised by this and asked multiple times how it was that God could weep. After all, He is the God over all; He knows the end from the beginning. Enoch reasoned that Heavenly Father had created numberless souls, many of whom chose the right, so how could He weep over this one group He was showing to Enoch (Moses 7:28–31)?

God's answer so tenderly shows His love for each and every one of us and also how much He values our own freedom to choose. He told Enoch, "Behold these thy brethren; they are the workmanship of mine own hands, . . . and in the Garden of Eden, gave I unto man his agency" (verse 32). He then explained that with agency, He also gave the commandment to love one another and to choose Him (verse 33). But He would never *make* them choose Him, just as He will never force us to choose Him now—not because He doesn't care or doesn't love His children, but precisely the opposite: because He loves us enough to never take that precious gift of freedom of choice from us.

When His children didn't use their agency to choose Him, God (as any loving parent would) felt the pain of their choices. He lamented to Enoch, "But behold, they are without affection, and they hate their own blood" (Moses 7:33). He knew the results of their choices even before they did. And it hurt Him. In every-day language, it's as if He were saying to Enoch, "These are my children. I made them. I love them. The only thing I want is for them to choose me and come back home. But they won't. Instead of love, they are choosing hate. And I know they are going to have to live with those choices, and in the end it won't lead them to happiness." Yes, He is affected when we make wrong choices. But He still holds true to His guarantee of our agency. It will never be taken from us.

Because we chose to come to earth, we now have the *responsibility of choice*. We cannot sit back and play neutral; we left that ground eons ago. Upon making the covenant of baptism, we chose yet again to follow Him. It is part of our path back to heaven. We have been given the chance in this world to prove ourselves, to see if we would make choices that qualify us to go back to God's presence (see Abraham 3:25). In the end, it is up to no one else but us; we own the responsibility to choose. God will help us. He has given us the Holy Ghost, scriptures, prophets, the priesthood, righteous Church leaders, prayer, and other blessings—but ulti-mately it is our choice to believe in and follow God.

Nephi taught us that we are here, walking the path of life, to be agents to "act . . . and not to be acted upon" (2 Nephi 2:26). We can't ever avert the responsibility. It lies within each and every one of us, regardless of our situation. We have all been given the Light of Christ (Moroni 7:16), and it is our decision to use it or not.

Here is the kicker: Yes, we have moral agency. We have the freedom of choice. The key that most of us overlook, however, is the accountability part. We are free to choose, but by choosing, we bind ourselves to the *results of our choices*.

Elder Marvin J. Ashton stated, "Our freedom to choose our course of conduct does not provide personal freedom from the consequences of our performances. God's love for us is constant and will not diminish, but he cannot rescue us from the painful results that are caused by wrong choices."[3] Or as Elder Todd D. Christofferson taught us, if we choose to not believe the law of gravity and step off a cliff, we will still, as a result of our choice, fall.[4]

I would like to share a personal story. It has come to be known in our house as The Parable of the Wand.

Years ago, we planned a trip to Disney World and Universal Studios in Florida. The kids were over-the-top excited; they could hardly wait. We planned for each child to have an allotment of spending money, but we told them that when it was spent, it was gone.

They were into Harry Potter, and for months, all they could talk about was getting a wand at Harry Potter World. That was the only thing they wanted from the whole trip—that beautiful, magical wand. They imagined, planned, talked, and dreamed about holding that amazing wand in their hands.

The time finally came for the trip. The schedule was three days in Disney World and the last day at Harry Potter World (wand nirvana).

If you've ever been to any Disney Park, you know how many rides conveniently exit right into the gift shop, where you are suddenly inundated with every souvenir you can possibly imagine that matches exactly the great ride you just experienced. Our young children's wait-for-the-wand willpower was no match for the bright lights and flashy toys. Instantly upon exiting each ride, the pleas started.

"Mom, I want to get this lightsaber."

"Are you sure? I thought you were going to save your money for the wand. And you already have *three* lightsabers at home."

"Not like *this* one! I have to get it! I'll still have money left for the wand. Please can I get it?"

And so went the cries. After every single ride. At one point, I kneeled down in front of one of the children, trying to come between him and the toy that was calling his name. I put my hands gently on his shoulders, looked into his eyes, and said, "I know and you know that you want the wand. It's all you have talked about. If you spend your money now, you won't be able to get that wand. You will be so sad. I don't want you to be sad. Please don't spend your money now." He then explained to me why he was convinced this toy he had in front of him now would be so much more fun than the wand that lay in the distant future. He took out his money and bought it.

The three days passed quickly. The new toys got old and lost their luster. We started our final day—the grand finale—in Harry Potter World. The kids eagerly sought out the wand shop. Much to their disappointment, they did not have enough money to buy the wand. They had all spent their money on other toys that seemed fun at the time. When they laid eyes on the wand, however, they realized that this, indeed, was what their hearts had truly wanted all along. But their choices had led them down a path where they could no longer afford it.

They begged. They pleaded. They bargained. My mother's heart broke. I wanted to go back on our agreement and get them each a wand anyway. But we had made a deal together and set up rules and guidelines, to which they had eagerly agreed. I had to stay consistent to the plan. I knew they had made choices that were not in harmony with their true desires, and now they had to be held accountable for those choices.

What had promised to be a fantastic ending to a dream vacation instead turned into a day of regret and remorse as they realized all too late that they had squandered their valuable dollars on the flashy here and now and let go of their longer vision.

The moral of this parable is summed up perfectly in Elder Richard G. Scott's message: "Don't give up what you most want in life for something you think you want now."[5] Every choice we make has a consequence.

Have you ever watched a scary movie, the kind that makes you jump in your seat? You know the type: There's a scary person behind the door. The girl goes to open the door. You scream at the TV, "Don't go in!" Why? Because you know the result of her choice to go in that door before she pushes it open. Sometimes I think the angels around us are screaming at us to not go through certain doors in life because they can see the results of some of our choices before we do. We either don't know what they will be, don't think far enough ahead, or perhaps don't think we will care.

There is a corny but catchy song titled "Choosing" on the sound track of *My Turn on Earth*. (Haven't heard of it? Go listen to it right now!) It talks about the fact that when we choose the first step on the road, we also choose the last.[6] That's how it is with choices: the consequence of the choice is bound to the decision we make.

Don't misunderstand. Repentance is real. It is full. It can take away the spiritual stain of any sin. The song goes on to tell us that if we don't like the end of the road, we better back up, and do it fast. Yes, repentance will cleanse you internally of any and all sins, regardless of how grave. The Atonement is there to help us erase the spiritual consequences of our sins through repentance. But it won't take away the natural consequences of the act of the sin. You can't unspeak hurtful words or gossip. You can't untell a lie.

Satan would have you think otherwise. He would have you think that in making whatever choice you want, you don't have to come face-to-face with the consequences of those choices. Look at abortion. In many cases, it stems from people not wanting to deal with the consequences of their immorality. Through abortion, they mistakenly believe they can get rid of the evidence of their choices and thereby remove themselves from the responsibility. What he doesn't tell them is that the sin was doubled from one of immorality to one of immorality and murder. And make no mistake—the consequences will come. I have spoken to and read about many women who chose to have an abortion. Years later, they still hang on to the pain and the guilt they never thought would come from that seemingly "quick and easy" solution.

This is part of the cunning of Satan. In lying to get you to believe there are no true consequences to your decisions, he tries to tempt you to make decisions that will actually remove your agency as you become subject to him (see Alma 12:17). How can this be possible, you ask? By using your agency to push a few simple buttons on a computer to view pornography (something he slyly whispers in your ear is not hurting anything or anyone), you soon find yourself addicted and a slave to the pornography industry. What you may say to yourself is a one-time thing of "just trying out" alcohol, drugs, smoking, or any other habit-inducing substance can soon bind you in the shackles of substance addiction. You will eventually realize you can no longer simply choose your way out of it without help from outside sources. What you may think is simply a diet to get the "perfect body" may soon turn into an obsessive eating disorder that can damage your internal organs, causing you problems for the rest of your life.

These are real-life examples of what Nephi called the "flaxen cord" (2 Nephi 26:22). A flaxen cord is a light yarn. When caught within the seemingly harmless snare of this thin string, you might not mind too much. However, as you travel deeper down the path of sin, this flaxen cord becomes thicker and thicker; you are so wrapped up in this sin that has possessed you that you discover a *decrease in your ability to free yourself*, even if you want to do so. Picture the shackles of substance addiction—or worse and more powerful, the prison of pornography. (You can take away alcohol or drugs, but you can't get away from those destructive images that are permanently etched in your mind.)

Do you see now how Satan twists truth so we think we are choosing freedom when really we are choosing captivity (see 2 Nephi 2:27–29)? Remember, however, the words of James E. Faust: "We need not become paralyzed with fear of Satan's power. He can have no power over us unless we permit it. He is really a coward, and if we stand firm, he will retreat. The Apostle James counseled: 'Submit yourselves therefore to God. Resist the devil, and he will flee from you' (James 4:7)."[7]

Satan is cunning. He has had thousands of years of experience in the trade of lying and betrayal. No one is exempt from his whisperings and temptations, especially not you—the future leaders of the Church and the world, and most important, the future nurturers and teachers of our Father's children. He is out to get the best, the elect of God (see Matt 24:24). He is out to get you. Don't let him in, not even for a second! Please always remember Sister Dew's directive to "shun him like the snake that he is."[8]

I remember once in seminary my teacher pulled out a stack of *Ensign* magazines. He had someone come up to the front of the room and put out one of her arms. He then proceeded to put one magazine at a time into her hand as we talked about each of the rules and laws we obey as members of the Church and about how they can seem restrictive to us. We keep the law of chastity. We keep the Word of Wisdom; we don't drink, we don't smoke, and we don't do drugs. We believe in honesty. The list went on, and we were feeling rather restrained by all of these rules.

Then came the zinger. He had her hold out her other arm. He got out a pile of incredibly thick books. He then started listing examples of consequences we experience when we choose not to abide by the rules. Suzie didn't keep the law of chastity, and she got pregnant at sixteen. *Boom*. Big book in the hand. Then Suzie decided to drink, got drunk, and drove, ultimately killing another person. *Boom*. Big book on the pile. Suzie stopped being honest, started to steal, and got caught and put in jail. *Boom*. Another big book. I could go on, but I think you get the point. Suddenly, the tiny paper *Ensign* magazines didn't seem so restrictive after all.

Elder Mervyn B. Arnold of the Seventy told a story that further illustrates this point. I have come to call this the "Don't Be a Stupid Cow" lesson. When his wife, Devonna, was a teenager, she felt the gospel rules were just way too restrictive—perhaps like some of you. She was working one summer on her dad's farm, and it was her job to help with the cows. They had a fence around the nice, green pasture to keep the cows out of the wheat fields. If the cows ate the wheat, they would bloat, possibly killing them.

One cow was constantly sticking her head through the fence, trying to see what was in the big, wide-open field and trying to get to the wheat. One morning, Devonna came out to see that the cow had broken through the fence and had eaten the wheat. By the time the girl came, the cow was in serious peril. Her first thought was, "You stupid cow! That fence was there to protect you, yet you broke through it and . . . your life is in danger." She ran to get her dad, but when they made it back, it was too late—the cow had died.[9]

Can you see the parallel here? Can you feel the Spirit sometimes whispering in your ear, "Don't be a stupid cow! The fences are here to protect you, not to restrict you. They are here to make you free, not to bind you"?

Your everyday "decisions do determine destiny."[10] President Hinckley taught, "The course of our lives is not determined by great, awesome decisions. Our direction is set by the little day-to-day choices which chart the track on which we run."[11] President Monson clarifies by adding that some decisions "will make no difference in the eternal scheme of things, and others will make all the difference."[12] For example, Elder Dallin H. Oaks gave great counsel we can heed every day. When we're faced with decisions, he advised us to ask the question, "Where will it lead?"[13] This is such a simple way to determine if your choices are taking you closer to or farther away from God. We can use this instruction immediately. Many of us mistakenly think our decisions to sin will only come back to haunt us when we face Judgment Day, giving us plenty of time to repent and "come around." But this question—"Where will it lead?"—can help us rethink some not-so-smart decisions by looking ahead a few hours, days, or years from now. For example, if someone has a goal to run a marathon but decides to turn the alarm off every morning when it comes time to train for the big day, what will happen come race time?

On the spiritual spectrum, if you choose to open your scriptures and study, even if it's merely for a few moments each day, by the time you graduate high school, you will have a whole reservoir of scriptures to help you in times of need. Yes, simply asking yourself where each decision will lead can help make many decisions a hundred times easier.

Your choices today determine your tomorrow. Elder Jeffrey R. Holland illustrated this vital fact. "In this battle between good and evil, you cannot play for the adversary whenever temptation comes along and then expect to suit up for the Savior at temple and mission time as if nothing has happened. That, my young friends, you cannot do. God will not be mocked."[14]

Elder Holland goes on to say that if you are already keeping the commandments (in other words, you're already on the team), then stay on the team. He warns: "Stop dribbling out of bounds just when we need you to get in the game and play your hearts out! In almost all athletic contests of which I know, there are lines drawn on the floor or the field within which every participant must stay in order to compete."[15]

So it is with God. Play within the lines. Why do you work so hard to stay within the lines at athletic events yet balk at keeping the rules within the Church?

I grew up playing sports, and volleyball was my passion through high school. In this game, one of the key rules is keeping the ball from hitting the floor on your side of the court. Countless hours were spent on that court, doing drill after drill purposefully aimed at trying every which way to keep that ball in bounds and in play. I never once had a coach say, "Now when you spike the ball, aim right for the line. See how close you can keep it to the line without actually going out." I think I still have some scars from all of the dives, lunges, and rolls I performed simply in the name of obeying the key rule—keep the ball in play. Yes, in the sports world, championships are won and lost based largely on keeping the ball in the right place. Why don't we view our own spiritual battle like that? Why don't we do all we can to stay securely within the spiritual bounds but instead see how close we can get to the edge?

Another way to gauge your choices is to ask yourself, "Is this choice going to help me get back home?" Some choices, like the choice between wearing a green or blue shirt, probably won't matter. Other choices will matter a great deal. If the choice you are about to make will truly impede you from returning home, then why would you want to make it? In the end, *nothing else* matters. And I guarantee you will be living on the other side a whole lot longer than you will be living here. Remember the yarn exercise? That's a long time to live with regret for some poor choices made here. William Law summed it up perfectly: "If you have not chosen the Kingdom of God first, it will in the end make no difference what you have chosen instead."[16]

Ultimately you must rely on the Holy Spirit and then place your faith in God to guide you to and along the path you need to choose. Sometimes He will wait for you to decide, to practice your agency, before confirming your decision or directing you a different way. Sometimes it will be a choice between two good options, and either is acceptable before God. He will let you know. Trust Him to do so (see Proverbs 3:5–6).

Some people think your choices only affect you, so why should it matter what you choose as long as you're okay with the consequences? It matters so much more than you may know. Bishop Richard C. Edgley talked about this when he shared the story of a man he knew who was less active for many years. The man had since made his way back to the gospel and worked in the temple with his wife. Bishop Edgley remarked, "All is well that ends well." The man responded, "No, all is not well. I am back in the Church, but I have lost all of my children and my grandchildren. And I am now witnessing the loss of my great-grandchildren—all out of the Church. All is not well."[17] How heartbreaking to realize all too late that our "personal" or "private" decisions are not as personal or private as we might think.

Among the choices we all have to make in life, there will be wrong choices—some large, some small—that inevitably take us away from our path back home.

That is precisely why our loving Heavenly Father gave us repentance. Repentance works. It is real. It can bring us back home. It is vital for us. None of us can make it back without this great gift from God brought to us through Jesus Christ. Elder

Richard G. Scott lovingly reminded us, "Remember, repentance is not punishment. It is the hope-filled path to a more glorious future."[18]

Isn't that incredible? Repentance is a glorious gift, not a painful punishment. Satan would have you think it's the latter. One of his best tactics is to tell you that once you are off the path there truly is no way back. "You aren't worthy," he says. "How can you expect to ever be made whole again? There's no way Heavenly Father would ever take you back now."

Don't listen to that. Don't buy in to Satan's lies. No matter how far down a wicked path you think you are, you always have the power to choose to come back. You will need help from the Savior, but you can always come back.

When we choose to repent and correct our poor choices, the Atonement of Christ allows God, through His mercy, to forgive those sins and remember them no more. While the natural or mortal consequences of our choices may stand unchanged (if we steal, we may have legal consequences that repentance cannot change), God can erase the spiritual price of justice, and we can once again be clean.

Let's look at Alma and the sons of King Mosiah. They not only made some bad choices for themselves, but they also set about trying to get other people to make the same choices, so much so that they were a great hindrance to the work of the Lord. They were so far off the beaten path that it took an angel of the Lord to come down and stop them. He told Alma that his choice now was to either stop seeking to destroy the Church or be cast off (Mosiah 27:16). That's quite the choice!

You know the story. He was struck down and went through some tough times in remembering all of his sins and poor choices. But then came a change. Let's look at how he described it. In Alma 36:17–18, he says that he was racked with torment, and then he remembered Jesus. He called on Him in his thoughts. "And now, behold, when I thought this, I could remember my pains no more. . . . And oh, what joy, and what marvelous light I did behold; yea, my soul was filled with joy as exceeding as was my pain!" (Alma 36:19–20).

That doesn't sound like the lament of someone who was too far gone for Christ to save. You are never too low for Christ to reach you. Remember, "he descended below all things" (D&C 88:6). Even if you feel like you have made too many bad choices, you still have the choice to stop and come back. I promise Christ is waiting with open arms to encircle you in His love.

Elder Holland reiterates this principle with his ever-poetic words, "However far from home and family and God you feel you have traveled, I testify that you have not traveled beyond the reach of divine love. It is not possible for you to sink lower than the infinite light of Christ's Atonement shines."[19]

As you travel through the many roads of life, please remember to make your choices count and, in all things, choose God and "the good part" (2 Nephi 2:30).

POINTS TO PONDER FROM CHAPTER 12

You may choose to ponder and pray about each concept as you answer the questions below. Plan how you can strengthen and build your testimony and act upon the principles you have studied.

Read Ether 12:27; James 4:7; and D&C 88:6.

Where is my path of choices taking me? Am I on the Lord's side "at all times and in all things, and in all places"?

_____

_____

_____

_____

_____

_____

_____

_____

How do my actions coincide with God's eternal goals and desires for me and who He wants me to become? How can I submit my will to God's?

_____

_____

_____

_____

_____

_____

_____

Am I worthy of the guidance of the Holy Spirit? How do I listen for and follow the Holy Ghost as I make decisions?

_____

_____

_____

_____

_____

_____

_____

What is my testimony of the Atonement of Jesus Christ?

_____

_____

_____

_____

_____

_____

_____

WE ARE DAUGHTERS OF OUR HEAVENLY FATHER

When I sin, am I filled with hope in the Atonement or despair that I will never make it back to God? What feelings do Christ and His endless atoning sacrifice offer to those who have sinned?

_____

_____

_____

_____

_____

_____

_____

_____

For further insight on choice and accountability, see:

- Neal A. Maxwell, "'Swallowed Up in the Will of the Father,'" *Ensign*, November 1995;
- M. Russell Ballard, "O That Cunning Plan of the Evil One," *Ensign*, November 2010;
- James E. Faust, "'The Great Imitator,'" *Ensign*, November 1987;
- James E. Faust, "Acting for Ourselves and Not Being Acted Upon," *Ensign*, November 1995;
- Thomas S. Monson, "The Three Rs of Choice," *Ensign*, November 2010;
- *Teachings of Presidents of the Church: David O. McKay* (Salt Lake City: The Church of Jesus Christ of Latter-day Saints, 2011), 204–13;
- Marvin J. Ashton, "A Pattern in All Things," *Ensign*, November 1990;
- Dallin H. Oaks, "Where Will It Lead?" *BYU Speeches*, November 9, 2004;
- Mervyn B. Arnold, "What Have You Done with My Name?" *Ensign*, November 2010;
- Gordon B. Hinckley, "Watch the Switches in Your Life," *Ensign*, January 1973;
- Jeffrey R. Holland, "We Are All Enlisted," *Ensign*, November 2011;

- Richard G. Scott, "Jesus Christ, Our Redeemer," *Ensign*, May 1997;
- Richard G. Scott, "Personal Strength through the Atonement of Jesus Christ," *Ensign*, November 2013;
- Jeffrey R. Holland, "The Laborers in the Vineyard," *Ensign*, May 2012.

Chapter 13

GOOD WORKS

"Therefore let your light so shine before this people, that they may see your good works and glorify your Father who is in heaven." (3 Nephi 12:16)

ON THEIR QUEST for values to add to the Young Women theme, Sister Kapp and the rest of the presidency searched in the book of Enos and noticed over and over that it is about Enos reaching out and caring for all of those around him, not just his friends and family but also his enemies. Then they read in Luke 22:32 the following instruction, "When thou are converted, strengthen thy brethren." These scriptures, among many that teach us to serve others, inspired them to add good works to the theme. This value is all about reaching out to help others.

According to Elder Robert C. Gay, the charge to keep the commandments of God is "more than just not doing bad things. . . . Taking upon the countenance of God means serving each other."[1] Likewise, President Monson admonished us to "never let a problem to be solved become more important than a person to be loved."[2]

It's not enough to know—we need to do! This value is not called good *intentions*; it is called good *works*. We need to be actively engaged in being an agent for good. We need to serve each other. Before you think you don't have enough time, talents, or energy to serve—or that it requires some grand gesture and scheduled service project—think about this: most of Christ's miracles were performed as He was on His way somewhere else to do something else. He didn't have people schedule appointments during designated hours He dedicated to His "good works" time slot. He did what needed to be done in the moment and on the spot to help someone. At one point in time, this even involved healing a sick man who was lowered through the roof of a house while he was engaged in another task (see Mark 2:1–12). Many of those things didn't take a lot of time, nor did they constitute some grand, extravagant gesture.

The following quote from Sister Chieko Okazaki, a former counselor in the Relief Society general presidency, is one of my all-time favorites:

> Remember Jesus healing the blind beggar. He spat on the ground, rubbed the mud on the man's eyes, and said, "Go, wash [your face] in the pool of Siloam" (John 9:1–7).
>
> My sisters, this story has a lesson about service in it for us. First, remember that Jesus and the man didn't have an appointment. They encountered each other almost by accident. So look for little opportunities in your daily life.
>
> Second, Jesus saw the need of an individual. Sometimes I think we see programs instead of individuals.
>
> Third, Jesus performed the service immediately with just the resources he had—spit and mud and a desire to help. He didn't transport the man to an exotic medical facility, organize a cornea transplant team, or didn't make it into a media event. Sometimes we think we can't serve because we're not rich enough, not educated enough, not old enough, or not young enough. Remember, if we have the desire to serve, then our bare hands, a little spit, and a little dirt are enough to make a miracle.[3]

Christ did things with just the resources He had. When you think in terms of service, *anything* is better than nothing. Often it can be doing what you do naturally. Smiling or saying hi could be just what someone needs at that moment. Too often we correlate good works with long, drawn-out service projects of pulling weeds, mowing lawns, or raking leaves. Yes, those are acts of service, and they are great activities to pursue. But just as significant could be putting your arm around someone in the hallway at school who is having a bad day. Listening to a friend is an act of service that is just as important. Paying for someone's lunch can be a small thing for you but a huge help for him. Slipping someone a note of encouragement could be just what she needs to carry on.

What can you do right here, right now to brighten someone's light around you? If you listen, you will hear, or feel, the vast need that is right within your reach.

Let me share a few examples. One night not long ago, we took our kids out to dinner for my husband's birthday. With our then six kids, we tended to make quite an entrance in the restaurant scene. In this particular restaurant, we were taken to a somewhat secluded area where there was just one other big table, which happened to be filled with adults who were clearly out to have an "adults only" night. As we came bounding in with our crew, we received some raised eyebrows from members of the other party. I felt a bit uncomfortable, just hoping that we could get through the dinner without any huge ordeal between the two completely opposite dinner parties. At the end of our meal, the waiter came with the check. Imagine our surprise when he informed us that an anonymous person at the other table had paid for our meal.

We had never met anyone at that table before, nor have we ever seen any of them since. We certainly hadn't done any great act to merit such a kindness. Some of the adults were quite annoyed by our very presence. Yet that act of kindness by one random person in the midst of them left a huge impression on our entire family. Truly there are still people in this world who go about doing good (see Acts 10:38).

The second example happened a few years ago when we were in the middle of a big snowstorm. It was a Saturday night, and we were ready to hunker down for the Sabbath. Out of the blue, I turned to my husband and told him that I was going to run to the gas station to grab some more milk. He looked at me like I was crazy and asked me why. (We had enough milk in the fridge to make it through until Monday). Equally puzzled myself by my declaration, I simply shrugged my shoulders and told him I didn't know, but I was going to go anyway.

I jumped into our Suburban and drove to the gas station. When I entered, there was an older couple using the gas station's phone, which I thought a bit strange in this world of cell phone abundance. I had a thought that they may need some help. (After all, who goes to the gas station to call someone just to catch up?) Not being one to pry into others' business, I tried to let it go and went to get my milk. As I approached the counter, however, I turned to the woman and asked if they needed any help. She grabbed her husband, and they explained that they lived at the top of a steep hill, and in the storm they couldn't make it with their car. They had left their cell phone at home, and their daughter who lived in town wasn't answering her phone. We all hopped in the trusty Suburban and easily made it up the hill to their house. I dropped them off, and we each went our separate ways. Our paths haven't crossed again.

This wasn't a life or death situation for me. It took all of ten extra minutes out of my day. I'm sure had I not been there, they would have made it home one way or another. As I drove home, I realized this act of service wasn't necessarily for them, but it was a huge lesson to me in how quickly and easily God will use us to help His other children, if we simply follow those promptings.

Neither of these examples made news headlines. Neither of them took any great strains of effort or time. Neither was earth shattering. However, they both left specific impressions that won't soon be forgotten.

Sharing our gifts and talents with others is another way to provide good works. In Doctrine and Covenants 46:12, God tells us that He specifically gives us different gifts "that all may be profited thereby." He purposefully divided the gifts between us so that we would have to work together to share those gifts. Many of us think of gifts only as those that can be shared in an outward "performance"—playing the piano, singing, speaking or writing well. But there are so many more that can be used to serve others. What personality gifts do you have? Do you have the ability to listen to someone? Do you have the gift of finding the positive? Do you have the gift of compassion? Many of these gifts of the Spirit can be used for the good and benefit of others; please take a look at Moroni 10:8–19 for more examples.

In this vast world of billions, it's easy to think that your contribution can't possibly make a difference. Elder M. Russell Ballard taught us how extremely important every tiny bit of service is through a comparison with honeybees. In a hive of 60,000 bees, all of them work their entire lifespan, and each individual contribution to the entire honey production is a mere one-twelfth of a teaspoon![4] Alone, that seems frustratingly insignificant. But collectively, they produce over 100 pounds of honey each season.[5] Elder Ballard went on to teach us that our individual service might seem insignificant, but as part of a collective whole, we can truly make a huge impact on the world for the better. Part of this big movement happens with a simple prayer: praying to find someone to serve today, then going about looking for ways to do good. The beauty of this is that it doesn't have to be a huge preplanned and highly organized Young Women value project. The tiny one-twelfth–teaspoon deposits *do* count!

If you pray for opportunities, be prepared, because they will come. I remember one day in college when I got really excited about the ability I had to make a difference for someone. I prayed for an opportunity to serve. What I didn't realize was that the opportunity would not necessarily come in my little time frame. I was right in the middle of midterms, had a test that day, and had a study group for another. In my mind, I had this little window of time I thought would work out perfectly for me to be able to help someone.

As you can probably guess, it didn't pan out quite that perfectly. Just as I was leaving to study before taking a test, I got a call from someone saying she was having a horrible day, that she really needed to talk to someone, and that my name came to her mind. I hate to admit it, but my first thought was, "Oh no. Not now,

Heavenly Father. This isn't what I prayed for. Didn't you hear the fine print in my prayer? I thought I stated I was available between two and three o'clock. This time frame doesn't fit at all with my schedule!" And then I almost laughed right out loud at myself. "Really? Was I just trying to dictate rendering service on my own selfish terms? Isn't that kind of a paradox?" That experience taught me a great lesson: when service comes up, it may not be the best time for you at the moment. But if you step out of yourself and choose to help another in need, I guarantee you will never regret having done so.

There are many different ways of giving small service. One popular adage is the "pay it forward" principle, where people simply do good works, and then when asked what they would like in return, they respond by asking the person to do a good turn for someone else. There are other programs where people participate in doing one act of service every day for thirty days without accepting or expecting anything in return. Think of how simple this would be: Incorporate one act once a day for thirty days. Think of that multiplied by millions of people who also take the service challenge. Suddenly your one-twelfth teaspoon has become an ocean of sweet honey. Every tiny bit of service matters. When we each add our bit to the jar, we can change the world. Now imagine what *two* acts a day could do.

Think of how many prayers could be answered simply by you going about doing good works. President Kimball taught, "God does notice us, and he watches over us. But it is usually through another person that he meets our needs. Therefore, it is vital that we serve each other."[6]

On the other hand, don't limit yourself. If you have great ambitions, big goals and plans to accomplish in the name of good works, go for it! If you go about it with God on your side and without giving up, you can achieve the big ideas you have in mind.

May I close this section with three phrases for you to think about? When you come upon a situation where you see a need for good works, don't brush off that gentle nudge of the Spirit prodding you to do something and give an excuse such as, "I don't have time," "I don't know what to do," or "I'm not an expert in what they need." Instead, ask yourself these simple questions:

1. If not now, then when?
2. If not here, then where?
3. If not me, then who?

And then let's all take the advice of President Hinckley's father to "forget [ourselves] and go to work."[7]

POINTS TO PONDER FROM CHAPTER 13

You may choose to ponder and pray about each concept as you answer the questions below. Plan how you can strengthen and build your testimony and act upon the principles you have studied.

What does "good works" mean? What kinds of things are "good works"?

_____

_____

_____

_____

_____

_____

_____

_____

What gifts of the Spirit do I possess? Which would I like to develop?

_____

_____

_____

_____

_____

_____

_____

What are my other talents? How will I develop them and use them to serve the Lord and His children?

_____
_____
_____
_____
_____
_____
_____
_____

How can doing good works help me to stand as a witness of God?

_____
_____
_____
_____
_____
_____
_____
_____

Who among my family members and friends would God have me serve?

_____
_____
_____
_____
_____
_____
_____
_____

How will I consistently strive to do good works?

_____
_____
_____
_____
_____
_____
_____
_____

For further insight on good works, study Matthew 25:40; 1 Corinthians 12:1–12; D&C 46:8–33; 58:26–29; and Moroni 10:8–18. See also:

- M. Russell Ballard, "Be Anxiously Engaged," *Ensign*, November 2012;
- Thomas S. Monson, "Anxiously Engaged," *Ensign*, November 2004;
- Robert D. Hales, "Gifts of the Spirit," *Ensign*, February 2002;
- Robert C. Gay, "What Shall a Man Give in Exchange for His Soul?" *Ensign*, November 2012;
- Thomas S. Monson, "Finding Joy in the Journey," *Ensign*, November 2008;
- Chieko Okazaki, "Spit and Mud and Kigatsuku," *Ensign*, May 1992;
- Spencer W. Kimball, "The Abundant Life," *Ensign*, July 1978.

Chapter 14

INTEGRITY

"God forbid that I should justify you: till I die I will not remove mine integrity from me." (Job 27:5)

WHAT IS INTEGRITY? What does it mean to have it? Elder Joseph B. Wirthlin said, "Integrity means always doing what is right, regardless of the immediate consequences. It means being righteous from the very depth of our soul, not only in our actions but, more importantly, in our thoughts and in our hearts."[1] In essence, it means living your testimony, not just bearing or saying it. It is doing what is right, even when no one will ever find out—perhaps *especially* when no one will ever find out.

I love how the Lord puts it. In the Doctrine and Covenants, He talks about the Prophet Joseph Smith's older brother: "Blessed is my servant Hyrum Smith; for I, the Lord, love him because of the integrity of his heart, and because he *loveth* that which is right" (D&C 124:15; emphasis added). I find it interesting that God said Hyrum "*loveth* that which is right," not "he *doeth* that which is right." Is it good to do the right? Of course. But here's the thing: you can do right while not loving the right. We can all act the part of the "good Mormon." But if we *love* the right, then God knows the natural result will be obedience (see Isaiah 29:13).

We will, through our love, always try to do those things that will bring us close to God.

Integrity is so much more than doing good. It is *being* good. Years ago, Paul Harvey, a famous news commentator, visited a school campus owned by the Church. After the visit, he stated, "Each . . . young face mirrored a sort of . . . sublime assurance. These days many young eyes are prematurely old from countless compromises with conscience."[2] One of the greatest blessings of integrity is never having to compromise your conscience. How liberating that is.

Clayton Christensen, an area authority in the North America Northeast area, gave a great illustration of the freedom of not having to compromise with your conscience. He tells a story of his college years at Oxford University in England, where he was the starting center on the basketball team. They had an undefeated season and went to the national tournament. They played well and made it to the finals. Much to his horror, he looked at the schedule and discovered the championship game was to be played on a Sunday.

He had decided many years ago, at the age of sixteen, that he would never play basketball on Sunday. As discussed earlier, when you make a decision once ahead of time, you don't have to keep remaking the decision. For Elder Christensen, this was one of those moments where the ideal of his teenage years' decision met with true integrity in his actions. This is where many people would jump in and say, "Just this once won't make a difference." It was no different in this scenario. His coach and teammates all pressured him to play in the game. His coach told him that God would understand the importance of this situation and playing with his team. His teammates were stunned that he would even consider letting them down in this way to appease his God.

He prayed about this decision and once again got a clear answer that he needed to hold strong to his commitment to the Lord. As Sunday dawned, he got up, got dressed, and attended his Church meetings, while his teammates played in the final game.

In his own words, Elder Christensen describes the importance of keeping true to himself and to his God:

> In theory, surely I could have crossed over the line just that one time and then not done it again. But looking back on it, I realize that resisting the temptation of "in this one extenuating circumstance, just this once, it's okay" has proved to be one of the most important decisions of my life. Why? Because life is just one unending stream of extenuating circumstances. . . . If you give in to "just this once." . . . you'll regret where you end up. . . . It's easier to hold to your principles 100 percent of the time than it is to hold to them 98 percent of the time. . . . Decide what you stand for. And then stand for it all the time.[3]

In short, integrity activates the previous values. It is all about making your actions and your life consistent with what you know in your heart, staying true to that knowledge for the long haul.[4]

POINTS TO PONDER FROM CHAPTER 14

You may choose to ponder and pray about each concept as you answer the questions below. Plan how you can strengthen and build your testimony and act upon the principles you have studied.

Do my dos and bes mirror one another? If not, what can I do to bring them more in alignment with one another?

_____

_____

_____

_____

Am I honest in my dealings with my fellow men? Can I improve my integrity in my thoughts and in my heart?

_____

_____

_____

_____

What does it mean to "compromise with conscience"? How will I avoid doing this?

_____
_____
_____
_____
_____
_____
_____
_____

What decisions will I make now so I don't compromise later?

_____
_____
_____
_____
_____
_____
_____
_____

An internal question to ask yourself comes from God's description of Hyrum Smith: Do I love that which is right?

For further insight on integrity, see:

- Neal A. Maxwell, "'According to the Desire of [Our] Hearts,'" *Ensign*, November 1996;
- Dallin H. Oaks, "Desire," *Ensign*, May 2011;
- Lynn G. Robbins, "What Manner of Men and Women Ought Ye to Be?" *Ensign*, May 2011;
- Joseph B. Wirthlin, "Priceless Integrity," *New Era*, July 1994;
- Clayton M. Christensen, James Allworth, and Karen Dillon, *How Will You Measure Your Life?* (New York: HarperCollins, 2012).

VIRTUE

"Who can find a virtuous woman? for her price is far above rubies." (Proverbs 31:10)

JUST AFTER SISTER Dalton, Sister Cook, and Sister Dibb were called to the general Young Women presidency in early 2008, they climbed to Ensign Peak and looked out over the valley. They posted a banner—a call for a return to virtue.[1]

On November 28, 2008, a letter from the First Presidency to all of the units in the Church announced the addition of *virtue* to the Young Women theme. The letter reads, in part: "This addition will assist young women in developing high moral standards. We invite parents and leaders to teach the doctrine of chastity and moral purity to help each young woman to be virtuous and worthy to make and keep sacred covenants and receive the ordinances of the temple."[2]

In many ways, this is not so much a brand new addition as an emphasis on the sacredness and absolute importance of virtue. Sister Dalton explained that the reason for the new value has everything to do with the temple, "and the temple is the reason for everything we are doing in Young Women, because it will help [us] to come unto Christ."[3] At the end of the day, the temple is where we want to be. It is our gateway into heaven. And one of the prerequisites to entering the Lord's holy temples is virtue.[4]

In *Preach My Gospel*, we learn virtue "is a pattern of thought and behavior based on high moral standards."[5] Sister Dalton explained, "It encompasses chastity and moral purity. . . . It is the accumulation of thousands of small decisions and actions. . . . The Latin root word *virtus* means strength."[6] To be virtuous is not to be a pious wallflower; it is to be a strong symbol of righteousness and moral values. Sister Dalton went on to say that people who have virtue possess a quiet dignity and inner strength.[7]

When you live virtuously, it is empowering to know you are worthy to be guided by the Holy Ghost at all times. We all desperately need this constant companionship to navigate around the devilish detours on the path back to heaven.

If you listen, the call to virtue can be heard above the raucous mocking of the world. It can even be heard from those young women who have gone long before us. One such voice was recorded in a written account from Lena Jensen, a young woman living in Moroni, Utah, in 1884. Her sweet, pure words echo through the centuries:

> My dear sisters, let us try to be virtuous. There is nothing that will bring us a greater reward than virtue. If we are virtuous and pure in the eyes of our Heavenly Father He will pour his blessings upon us. Let us make up our minds to be virtuous . . . for virtue is better than riches. My dear sisters, how blessed we are if we will only live as we should. . . . Let us cultivate the faculties which our Heavenly Father has given us so that when we are called to leave this stage of action . . . God may say, well done thou good and faithful servant, enter in to my glory and be clothed in robes of righteousness.[8]

It is so fitting that virtue comes at the end of the theme, for it is the culmination of all the other values. Living a virtuous life is truly how you, as a young woman, can put on your beautiful robes and enter into the house of the Lord, unspotted and ready to be endowed from on high to receive all the blessings that Heavenly Father is waiting to bestow upon you.

Preparing and preserving your virtue is not just a good idea, not just one more lesson to be learned in Young Women, it's critical—even vital—to the plan of salvation. The power of pro-creation is how you become an integral part of carrying out this plan, by forming the bodies God's spirit children can come in for their life on earth.

Have you ever wondered why God lists two of the most griev-ous of sins as murder and sexual immorality (see Alma 39:5)? These two sins are directly linked to the bookends of life—the taking and the giving of it. To do either in a way contrary to the plan of God brings with it much sorrow and heartache. The value of life is sacred; it is one of the foundational principles of the plan of salvation. Not respecting the value or sacredness of life is truly trampling on this plan.

It is ironic that Satan has turned virtue on its head with his flattering words and the virtue-is-old-fashioned mentality he has embedded so cleverly into our modern-day society. Let's take a look at some sobering statistics about moral virtue.

On average, 46 percent of all high school aged students have had sex. By the time they graduate, that number jumps to 62 per-cent.[9] Think you won't find peer pressure to put down your virtue? Think again.

President Hinckley has told us that choosing your spouse will "be the most important decision of your life."[10] Elder Bruce R. McConkie, former member of the Quorum of the Twelve, even took this a step further when he stated, "The most important single thing that any Latter-day Saint ever does in this world is to marry the right person, in the right place, by the right authority."[11] In light of the enormous importance of this decision, why would you want to jeopardize it by giving in too soon and giving away your virtue? In contrast, if you just wait a bit, you won't lose your virtue; instead you will share it with your husband and helpmeet, the most important person in your life.

We all have a naturally ingrained instinct that drives us to procreate. This is normal. In fact, it's a God-given response for the act of intimacy. The huge difference between the righteousness and wickedness of it lies not in the act itself but in following the Master's command and going about it in His way.

We are counseled in the Book of Mormon to put "off the natural man" and to become "willing to submit to all things which the Lord seeth fit to inflict upon [us], even as a child doth submit to his father" (Mosiah 3:19).

Waiting for marriage to share sexual relationships will be one of the greatest gifts you ever give your husband, yourself, and even your future children. I know it's hard. I know it's frustrating to have to keep turning away and standing up to temptation now. The reason you are counseled to shun sex now is not because it is something awful and horrible. It's just the opposite. It is so powerful and so incredible that it truly can bind two people together in a way that no other act can.

Sexual feelings are not evil or bad in themselves. They are natural. It's not a matter of never experiencing those feelings; rather, it is vital to wait until the right time, not dwelling on them and never doing anything to encourage them until the right time.[12] In other words, even though the drive is there, it is our choice to look away from the desire and instead focus intently God and wait for His directive. In putting off the natural-man instincts for a season, we can then enjoy the reward of this great experience with no guilt or remorse whatsoever.

You aren't "missing out." I promise you, it's everything to the contrary. You are saving such a sacred act for committed matrimony. And once you have made those eternal covenants with your celestial partner, you can then share that part of yourself with him for the rest of your life, and that will be worth so much more than a one-night stand or a sexual relationship built outside of marriage. The same act, when performed prematurely, is a grievous sin. But when performed at the right time, after making the right covenants, it is an incredibly spiritual experience.

No, you aren't missing out by being virtuous. You are winning the battle against Satan and will save yourself much heartache by living in purity.

How can the same act be so utterly wicked at one time and so sacred in another? The difference is the marriage—a committed relationship and divine institution bound by covenants. There will be no waking up with regret in the morning, no hating yourself for giving in to worldly pressure. There will just be utter and complete love—the way the Lord designed an intimate relationship to be.

It is so worth the wait. Believe me, when the right time comes, you will spend the rest of your life thanking your younger self for waiting. Elder D. Todd Christofferson reminded us in 2013 that for as long as history has been kept, societies have relied on the moral force of women.[13] How Satan is chipping away at that fortitude! Don't give in to it. Don't just avoid the worst things; elevate yourself above the crass to be classy. Don't just avoid immorality; stand up for morality. Stand strong for modesty. You are worth so much more than the trashy clothes that seem to be the latest styles.

Elder Christofferson goes on to say to the young women,

> Protect and cultivate the moral force that is within you. Preserve that innate virtue and the unique gifts you bring with you into the world. . . . Don't lose that moral force even before you have it in full measure. Take particular care that your language is clean, not coarse; that your dress reflects modesty, not vanity; and that your conduct manifests purity, not promiscuity. You cannot lift others to virtue on the one hand if you are entertaining vice on the other. . . . And do not be afraid to apply that influence without fear or apology.[14]

I love that last phrase, "without fear or apology." We don't have to apologize for staying true. Hold strong to your morals and values. It will only enhance your attractiveness to the type of man you will want to marry some day, the type of man with whom you want to raise children. "Virtue loveth virtue; light cleaveth unto light" (D&C 88:40). Simply by cleaving unto your virtue and light, you will attract the type of person with whom you will truly want to share eternity.

Remember the Articles of Faith? Remember that really long thirteenth one? (The one that you dreaded having to memorize?) "We believe in being honest, true, chaste, benevolent . . ." Is it starting to ring a bell? I love the ending: "If there is anything virtuous, lovely, or of good report or praiseworthy, we seek after these things" (Articles of Faith 1:13). See? If you wonder if being virtuous is going to cost you dates, think of it this way: by you staying virtuous, the young men you ultimately want will be seeking after you.

I do feel compelled to also address something rather difficult and heavy. The very thought of it makes me sad inside. This is the subject of rape. The sad truth is that there are many among our own young women who have endured, or who likely will endure, such a horrific act against their will. The statistics tell us that one out of six girls is sexually assaulted in her lifetime.[15]

In the case of sexual assault, many people report experiencing myriad feelings, including the feeling that they are now "damaged goods" and feelings guilt and shame, like it was somehow their fault. Others reported that they felt like they had lost a part of themselves.[16] One well-known victim of this horrible crime, Elizabeth Smart, stated how she felt, "I was broken beyond repair. I was going to be thrown away."[17] She also stated something that many who have gone through the same thing may also feel, "Oh, my gosh, I'm that chewed up piece of gum, nobody re-chews a piece of gum, you throw it away."[18]

Ann Pritt, a therapist and a member of The Church of Jesus Christ of Latter-day Saints, stated, "The gospel teaches that when bad things happen to people, this does not make *them* bad. No one can destroy another's possibilities for eternity. We are judged only for our own desires, intentions, and actions, not for the actions of others against us."[19]

If this is something that has happened to you, please know that first and foremost God loves you. You are still that $100 bill (see chapter 10). You are still His daughter. Your virtue is still 100 percent intact. I cannot even begin to imagine what you must be feeling. But I do know that in God's eyes, you are every bit as loved and pure as the day you left His side.[20]

Virtue is needed in this world. Cling to yours like you would cling to a lifeboat in a sea of raging water. If you feel you have let your virtue go, take the steps necessary to get it back. Do it now. The Young Women presidency offered a place to start: "Pray night and morning. Read in the Book of Mormon five minutes or more each day. And smile." Sister Dalton then went on to say, "If all women in the Church and the world did this, think what the world would be like in five years. We really do believe that virtuous young women led by the Spirit can change the world."[21]

POINTS TO PONDER FROM CHAPTER 15

You may choose to ponder and pray about each concept as you answer the questions below. Plan how you can strengthen and build your testimony and act upon the principles you have studied.

What is virtue? How is it more than just living the law of chastity?

_____

_____

_____

_____

How am I living virtuously now? How can I improve?

_____

_____

_____

_____

"Light cleaveth unto light." What kind of man do I want to be with for eternity? How will I live so that I can be worthy of and attractive to that type of person?

_____

_____

_____

_____

What compromising situations do I commit to avoid?

_____

_____

_____

_____

How can I be an example of virtuous living? How can I influence others to be virtuous, especially when it may not be popular? How will I commit now to be a guardian of virtue—my own and that of others?

_____

_____

_____

_____

For further insight on the importance of virtue, see Jacob 2:28; Moroni 9:9; and Articles of Faith 1:13. See also:

- *Gospel Principles* (Salt Lake City: The Church of Jesus Christ of Latter-day Saints, 2011), 224–32;
- "Sexual Purity," "Entertainment and Media," "Music and Dancing," and "Dating," in *For the Strength of Youth* (Salt Lake City: The Church of Jesus Christ of Latter-day Saints, 2011);
- David A. Bednar, "We Believe in Being Chaste," *Ensign*, May 2013;
- D. Todd Christofferson, "The Moral Force of Women," *Ensign*, November 2013;
- Robert L. Backman, "Chastity: The Source of True Manhood," *Ensign*, November 1989;
- James E. Faust, "The Virtues of Righteous Daughters of God," *Ensign*, May 2003;
- Jeffrey R. Holland, "Of Souls, Symbols, and Sacraments," BYU devotional address, 12 January 1988;
- Elaine S. Dalton, "A Return to Virtue," *Ensign*, November 2008;
- Gordon B. Hinckley, "Life's Obligations," *Ensign*, February 1999.

Chapter 16

WE BELIEVE AS WE COME
to Accept and Act
UPON THESE VALUES

CCEPTANCE IS THE first step in any spiritual development. One of the best ways you can accept the values
is to act upon the values. It is the movement toward
action that will enhance and strengthen the acceptance, just like
faith and works. (We believe, and then we work to show that
belief.) God teaches us this principle with the concept of tithing.
He even told us to "prove me now herewith" (Malachi 3:10). He
told us to try it, to follow the principle and see what blessings
would flow from heaven. If you are struggling with accepting,
then try this principle. In John 7:17, we learn that our testimonies
grow when we "do his will." Try the actions, because ultimately
we need to act, not just accept.

Sister Dalton stated her belief in you as a young woman: "I
truly believe that one virtuous young woman or young man, led
by the Spirit, can change the world, but in order to do so . . . [we]
must engage in strict training."[1] Notice she didn't say "engage in
strict acceptance." We must *do*. Juma Ikangaa, winner of the New
York Marathon in 1989, said, "The will to win is nothing without
the will to prepare."[2] We have to act, and we have to start now.

In the New Testament, James also tells us about the importance of action: "But be ye doers of the word, and not hearers only, deceiving your own selves. . . . Whoso looketh into the perfect law of liberty, and continueth therein, he being not a forgetful hearer, but a doer of the work, this man shall be blessed in his deed" (James 1:22, 25).

How many times have you been in a great Church meeting? You feel the Spirit. You feel motivated. You are ready to get out and make the changes needed to improve. And then you go home . . . and get right back into your regular routine.

Yep, sounds a lot like the rest of us. To know is one thing. To feel is another. To actually do the actions and make changes is a whole different story altogether. It's not easy. Real and lasting change is difficult and can be lonely at times, especially when those around you are so content to stay where they are. For example, in the story of Lehi's dream, those who wanted eternal life had to do more than just hear the word—they had to do more than even grab onto the iron rod. They had to *move*. And they had to keep moving, even through the darkness. In the end, those who made it had to hold fast and *continue* (see 1 Nephi 8:24, 30, 33). Christ Himself tells us directly, "Not every one that saith unto me, Lord, Lord, shall enter into the kingdom of heaven; but he that *doeth* the will of my Father who is in heaven" (3 Nephi 14:21; emphasis added).

Personal Progress is a great place to help us do this. The program was laid out specifically to help imprint these values into your hearts and minds. If you look at the program, each value has goals that help you study and learn about the value. Each value also has experiences that require action, which in turn helps you do and become as you truly internalize each of these core values.

The values are great to learn about. It's great to memorize the meaning and scriptures behind them, great to even make cute little crafts and hang them on your wall. But if all you do is look at them and then leave them hanging, literally and figuratively, you are deceiving yourself. You must hang them on your heart, have them with you everywhere, "at all times and in all things, and in all places." They are not a mere wall hanging, but together they form a cloak to protect you from "the fiery darts of the adversary" (1 Nephi 15:24). Much like a coat will keep you safe from the winter wind, these values, if properly worn and used, will keep you safe from the whirlwind of buffetings from Satan.

The values: read and learn them, and then live and exemplify them.

POINTS TO PONDER FROM CHAPTER 16

You may choose to ponder and pray about each concept as you answer the questions below. Plan how you can strengthen and build your testimony and act upon the principles you have studied.

What do I believe the Young Women values and Personal Progress can do for me? How can I choose to accept and act upon them in my life?

_____
_____
_____
_____
_____
_____
_____
_____

What can I do to gain a personal testimony of these values and to invite the Holy Ghost to help me act on them?

_____
_____
_____
_____
_____
_____
_____
_____

Will I let Personal Progress change me for the better? What do I need to do in order to change?

How will I live and exemplify the Young Women values?

For further insight on acting on what you know, study Mormon 7; 2 Corinthians 8:17; and John 7:17. See also:

- David A. Bednar, "Ask in Faith," *Ensign*, May 2008;
- Donald L. Hallstrom, "What Manner of Men?" *Ensign*, May 2014;
- David A. Bednar, *Increase in Learning* (Salt Lake City: Deseret Book, 2011);
- David A. Bednar, *Act in Doctrine* (Salt Lake City: Deseret Book, 2012).

Chapter 17

WE WILL BE PREPARED
to Strengthen
HOME AND FAMILY

WHEN I WAS in Young Women, this part of the theme hadn't yet been added. It was added in 2001 under the direction of Sister Nadauld. This was not a quick let's-add-it-in-just-because insertion. In a timely way, "strengthen home and family" was added after the family proclamation was announced. Sister Nadauld and her counselors understood the family's central role in God's plan, Satan's relentless attacks on the family in these latter days, and your role in strengthening and defending the family. They knew they needed to incorporate this into the theme. They tried many variations and put much thought, energy, prayer, and patience into this addition, wanting to ensure the final statement was truly inspired of God.[1] They knew it would be imprinted into your mind, so they wanted to get it right. Because you say them each Sunday, the four little words *strengthen home and family* become an integral part of the principles you will remember.

It's interesting that this line comes before making covenants in the temple. Usually when we think of home and family, we think of it in a future tense. But this placement tells us we don't need to wait until we have our own family in the future to begin strengthening. You can start right now, today, with the family in which you now reside. There is so much good and so much strength you can provide to your family now, even as a young woman.

You all come from unique family situations. For some of you, strengthening your family could be done by participating in family home evening and family scripture study. For others, it might be setting a good example for those who are struggling. It can be having a good attitude in family activities (even when it's the last place you want to be), or helping with younger siblings. The point is, strengthening your family can be anything, simple or grand, that you do with a purpose. You can turn from reacting to situations to helping proactively create a better family environment. (Remember that little value called good works?)

I will never forget one particular family home evening we had when I was in sixth grade. At the time, I basically idolized my four older brothers; they were my heroes. I was the youngest of seven kids, so you can imagine the lively family home evenings that happened within our walls. This particular night, one of my brothers, in high school at the time, was in charge of the lesson. The topic was "Families Are Forever." I cannot remember a single word of the lesson. What I do remember—indeed, what I will never forget—is this: At the end of the lesson, he walked up to each member of the family individually and handed us a little paper that had the words "Families Are Forever" written on it. He then looked at every one of us and said, "I want to live with *you* forever."

Can you imagine what this did to my young eleven-year-old self, to hear my big, cool brother look at me and tell me that he wanted to live with me forever? It was amazing. The lesson probably took him all of twenty minutes to prepare and about that long to present. It was a relatively small act for him to do this for the family. And yet, it resonated with me for years to come. Think you can't strengthen your family unit here and now? Think again. You can leave more of an impression on your siblings and parents than you may now imagine.

In addition to strengthening your families now, you may have the opportunity in the future to have your own family, whatever form that may be: just you and your husband, or with two kids, three kids, twelve kids, maybe a pet or two. This line, "we will be prepared to strengthen home and family," is to me one of the most important concepts we can learn and live as daughters of God. Why? I submit to you that home and family is the final battle-front. Satan has a hold on almost every other sphere in life. He has crept into almost every place we used to consider safe havens. Even schools are full of his influence.

Home and family are at the heart of the plan of salvation. If Satan can get inside our homes, then his job is close to complete. If he can destroy what modern prophets have called "the funda-mental unit of society,"[2] he doesn't have to work so hard on the peripherals. Look around you. Can you see it happening? Can you see his plan working? I can see it more so than I ever thought possible. We can take comfort in knowing that the Lord's plan is working too. And as long as we are following it with exactness in our homes and families, we will be able to withstand Satan's attack.

I think it's safe to say that the family is of great importance to God. It is *everything* to God. Look up "Temple" in the Bible Dictionary. The part that catches my eye is this: "A temple is liter-ally a house of the Lord. . . . A place where the Lord may come, it is the most holy of any place of worship on the earth. *Only the home can compare with the temple in sacredness*" (Bible Dictionary, "Temple"; emphasis added). Yes, you read that right: God com-pares the sacredness of the home to the *temple*.

Science and research are once again catching up with the rev-elations of God. We have long been told that family time should be protected and cherished. Now research is showing the huge benefit that can come from family time. In fact, having dinner together as a family has been proven to correlate with higher grades, lower drug use, and greater self-esteem.[3]

Dr. John Hittinger, a professor of philosophy at the University of St. Thomas stated, "The family represents nature in its clearest manifestation. . . . The family is said to be the basic cell of all human society, the primary association of human beings."[4] William Bennett, a former United States Secretary of Education, stated, "For a civilization to succeed, the family must succeed."[5]

Here are some interesting statistics on the family. Children born and raised in intact family units (with both a mother and a father in the home) score higher on reading skills as early as pre-school years and score higher in reading comprehension in fourth grade. They are 30 percent less likely to skip school or even be tardy. They are also two times more likely to graduate from high school. Children in intact households are less likely to experience depression or anxiety or to abuse alcohol or drugs. They are also less likely to think about or attempt suicide. Teenage pregnancy rates in intact household are 5 percent. That rate increases to between 10 and 35 percent in homes where the father is absent.[6]

The advantages are not only the children's. Women and men in traditional marriages live longer lives, experience less illness, show fewer signs of depression, and have a lower rate of drug and alcohol abuse than their single or even cohabiting counterparts.[7]

Perhaps one of the strongest societal calls for a return to traditional marriage and family comes from a series of studies performed by Harvard sociologist Robert Sampson, in which he concluded, "Family structure is one of the strongest, if not the strongest, predictor of variations in urban violence across cities in the United States."[8] In other words, his studies linked the increase in crime rate in the United States over the past several decades to the breakdown of the traditional family unit.

Of course Satan knows this. That is why he is working so hard on destroying this core of society. If he can lead you to devalue your role as a mother in Zion, if he can get the family unit to weaken and fall apart, then his job is so much easier.

Contrary to popular belief, striving to be a homemaker in your home is not outdated. It is not old fashioned. It is not hiding from the battles of the "real world." Quite the contrary, it is placing yourself at the forefront of the battle—arming the soldiers for the final showdown with Satan. What career in the world can you

WE ARE DAUGHTERS OF OUR HEAVENLY FATHER

think of that can have more of an influence on a human being than the gentle and constant teaching and care that come from a mother? None. Absolutely none.

Just as the armies of Helaman were prepared for battle when the time came, so must you prepare your home and children for war. Make no mistake about it, it *is* a war. Or rather, it's the continuation of the age-old war, begun before this life. In this war, there is so much more than physical life or death at stake. We are talking about eternal consequences. As I stated before, Satan comes at you with thousands of years of experience, while we as mothers and home guardians, comparatively, just got here to mortality. But do not ever underestimate the promises and power of God. We have Him on our side, and as long as we stay partners with Him, He will not let us fail. He will help us fulfill our calling as mothers.[9]

Let's revisit the story of the stripling armies of Helaman. Notice that they didn't have to take a crash course in how to rely on their God when they decided to go to battle. They immediately said they would go and do. And they gave all of the credit for their faith to their mothers: "They had been taught by their mothers, that if they did not doubt, God would deliver them" (Alma 56:47). Notice they didn't say their teachers taught them or their day care workers taught them; their *mothers* taught them.

Do you think these mothers knew when their children were young that their sons would choose to serve on the battlefront to help protect their people? Not at all—in fact these mothers were the same ones who helped their husbands bury their weapons of war and make a covenant of peace (see Alma 24:17–18). Preparing their sons for battle was probably the furthest thing from their minds. But they did prepare their sons to believe and trust in God. They gave their sons a foundation of strength that could be used to get them through whatever battle they needed to fight. Recall Helaman 5:12, the promise of the strength that comes from building "upon the rock of our Redeemer." That was what these mothers taught their children.

Prepare for and plan to be that kind of mother. Be the kind of mother who raises the army of Helaman. Although your children may never be called to the battlefront of a physical war, they absolutely will be continually engaged in the war with evil. And that is perhaps even more dangerous, for the enemy we fight now is not a tangible target across a literal battlefield. You must help your children fight the cunning and insidious influences Satan will place before them.

President Spencer W. Kimball explained, "To be a righteous woman during the winding up scenes on this earth, before the second coming of our Savior, is an especially noble calling. . . . She has been placed here to help to enrich, to protect, and to guard the home—which is society's basic and most noble institution."[10]

President Hinckley added, "You are the guardians of the hearth. You are the bearers of the children. You are they who nurture them and establish within them the habits of their lives. No other work reaches so close to divinity as does the nurturing of the sons and daughters of God."[11]

I love the use of the term *guardian*. By definition, a guardian is one who defends, protects, or keeps.[12] You are there to protect this precious family unit, to keep it safe, and to defend it against the army of Satan.

Does that mean you give up all your personal hopes and dreams? Absolutely not! You may need to alter or suspend them for a time while you embark on this journey of motherhood, but you don't lose yourself in motherhood. You develop your talents and increase your capacity in motherhood. You will learn lessons about providing for God's children that will also prepare you for godhood. You gain knowledge, and then you apply it to and share it in your home and family. In doing so, you can't help but grow more yourself. (It's another one of those cyclical processes.) Is it hard? Yes. If you become a wife and mother, it will be the hardest job you will ever have in this life. It will take all you have. And that's why it's so important to prepare now. Being neck-deep in dirty diapers and screaming babies is not the time to find your testimony of building home and family.

Strengthen home and family: four small words that you repeat each Sunday. Yet the meaning behind these words takes a lifetime, perhaps even an eternity, to fully comprehend and master. Start with one step. Start with where you are now. As you repeat these four words each week, resolve to do one thing in your current family or for your future family to help strengthen and preserve this eternally crucial God-given institution, the very core of society.

POINTS TO PONDER FROM CHAPTER 17

You may choose to ponder and pray about each concept as you answer the questions below. Plan how you can strengthen and build your testimony and act upon the principles you have studied.

What does it mean to "strengthen home and family"?

_____
_____
_____
_____
_____
_____
_____
_____

What helped women in the scriptures and in the early years of the restored Church to strengthen home and family?

_____
_____
_____
_____
_____
_____
_____
_____

What can I do to strengthen my current home and family?

_____

_____

_____

_____

_____

_____

_____

_____

What is my plan for strengthening my future home and family?

_____

_____

_____

_____

_____

_____

_____

_____

Why is motherhood a noble calling?

_____

_____

_____

_____

_____

_____

_____

_____

WE ARE DAUGHTERS OF OUR HEAVENLY FATHER

What do I want to teach my children? What knowledge and education must I gain to prepare to do so? How will I plan with my husband to strengthen home and family and teach our children the gospel of Jesus Christ?

_____
_____
_____
_____
_____
_____
_____

How will I prepare to engage in the fight against Satan in my youth and as a mother?

_____
_____
_____
_____
_____
_____
_____

For further insight on families and motherhood, study Alma 56. See also:

- "The Family: A Proclamation to the World," *Ensign*, November 1995, 102;
- *Gospel Principles* (Salt Lake City: The Church of Jesus Christ of Latter-day Saints, 2009), 207–23, especially chapter 37;
- Jeffrey R. Holland, "Motherhood: An Eternal Partnership with God," LDS.org, accessed May 2014. Available at https://www.lds.org/pages/motherhood;
- *Daughters in My Kingdom: The History and Work of Relief Society* (Salt Lake City: The Church of Jesus Christ of Latter-day Saints, 2011), especially chapter 9;

JEN BREWER

- Julie B. Beck, "Mothers Who Know," *Ensign*, November 2007;
- *Teachings of Presidents of the Church: Harold B. Lee* (Salt Lake City: The Church of Jesus Christ of Latter-day Saints, 2000), 109–45;
- Ezra Taft Benson, "The Honored Place of Woman," *Ensign*, November 1981.

MAKE AND KEEP
Sacred
COVENANTS

SISTER ARDETH G. Kapp said, "A good measurement to ask concerning every important decision is whether or not this decision will move you toward or away from making and keeping sacred covenants and preparing for the ordinances of the temple."[1]

Sister Linda K. Burton told us, "Making and keeping our covenants is an expression of our commitment to become like the Savior."[2] Covenants are vitally important to our salvation. Our covenants are what bind us to God and forge a path for us to return home to Him.

Let's return to the families of the armies of Helaman, the Anti-Nephi-Lehies (also known as the Ammonites—the people who were converted through the missionary efforts of Ammon). Long before the sons became the army of Helaman, their fathers were converted to the gospel. Their conversion was so complete that they buried their weapons of war and covenanted with God that they would rather die than shed blood again (Alma 24:18). They were then taken to live with the Nephites so they could be protected. Years down the road, however, the Lamanites attacked the Nephites again, and the people of Ammon were moved with compassion and wanted to help defend their brethren, the Nephites (Alma 53:13). They had the best of intentions. They didn't want to break their oath simply because they became blood thirsty again; they thought it was important to break their oath to be able to help defend the lives of their people (Alma 53:14).

How appropriate was Helaman's concern: "And Helaman feared lest by so doing they should lose their souls; therefore all those who had entered into this covenant were compelled to behold their brethren wade through their afflictions, in their dangerous circumstances at this time" (Alma 53:15). That is incredible to me. Here was a group of people who would have made a tremendous contribution to the army and would have helped defend the country and spare lives. But when comparing the physical and spiritual dangers we face, Helaman knew we must first defend our souls. He grasped the bigger picture that our covenants with God are much more critical to our salvation than physical threats.

Are you reading this with your spiritual eyes? Can you see the parallels to this in your life? Your covenants to God are worth so much more than not getting made fun of or harassed. You may even lose some friends and popularity along the way. Your covenants to God mean *everything*. Your covenants are what will seal you to Him and to eternal life. In the end, that is all that matters.

We can all read the end of this story: Helaman knew God would bless them in His own way, which they fully trusted. The sons of these families had not themselves entered into the peace covenant, so they rose and came to Helaman, making a covenant in the opposite extreme—to fight for the liberty of their land and people, even to the laying down of their own lives if needed (Alma 53:17). They didn't know if they would live or die when they marched into battle, yet because of their faith and full trust in God, they were ready to defend their families. They faced some rather daunting odds in the battles that ensued, but in the end, not one of the sons was killed.

Yes, when we keep our covenants and use our faith to take brave steps, God blesses us immensely. It may not be as dramatic as the story of the stripling warriors, but the blessings will come.

There are two distinct truths about life I would like to discuss. Truth #1: None of us is going to get out of life alive. Every single one of us, at some point in time, is going to die. Truth #2: We know who is going to win. In the end, after all Satan can do (and he can do a lot) to try to thwart the plan of God, it will be in vain. We have been told that over and over again. So really, the only question to ask yourself is, when all is said and done, whose side are you on? You may try to come up with a bunch of different scenarios to ask "What about this?" and "What if that?" But really, the only question that matters is whose side are you on? Since we don't know exactly when our turn to die will come (for some it will be as soon as tomorrow, for others it won't be for another ninety years), wouldn't it make sense to make sure we make our stand now and stick with it?

How do we make that stand? You guessed it—through covenants. Let's go back to truth #1: We are all going to die. Now think about this: In the final journey of the mortal body to be laid in the cemetery, there has never once been one transported with a luggage rack on the top of the hearse. Nobody has the ability to carry any physical object with him or her into the next life. If we can't take anything with us, then why do we waste our precious time and energy caring so much about those objects of the here and now?

So if we can't take anything physical with us, then what *do* we take? Knowledge, for one, and the relationships we have made while here on earth. How do we keep our family relationships after we die? How do we physically and spiritually stay together beyond the "till death do you part"? Through covenants. We make the sacred covenants with God that literally bind us to Him—not just for time on earth, but forever. These covenants make it possible to get back home to God with all of our loved ones.

Where do we make these covenants? The first we make is in the baptismal font, and it is renewed each Sunday when we partake of the sacrament. The rest—those beautiful, eternally reaching covenants—are made in the temple, the most holy place on earth.

Yes, we make covenants both in the baptismal font and in the temple, but where do we *keep* those covenants? It is in our day-to-day lives through our actions that we maintain our end of the deal. Prior to making covenants through sacred ordinances, we prepare to do so by making efforts to live in accordance with them in our childhood and youth. When we do make these holy promises, we commit to keep them everywhere—"at all times and in all things, and in all places." Once we walk out of the church or the temple, we are still under the obligation to keep our part of the covenants we have made. There is never a time when we are not required to keep them. There is never room for "just this once." Remember God's just warning in the last half of Doctrine and Covenants 82:10: if we don't keep our covenants, then He is no longer bound to His promises upon which our covenants are based.

No, this gospel is not one in which we pick and choose when and where we will obey. It is a Church of true discipleship, which is built by our daily decisions and actions. Making covenants is a one-time event. Keeping those covenants is a quest we continue to the end. President Uchtdorf summed it up perfectly: "Being a disciple of Jesus Christ is not an effort of once a week or once a day. It is an effort of once and for all."[3]

POINTS TO PONDER FROM CHAPTER 18

You may choose to ponder and pray about each concept as you answer the questions below. Plan how you can strengthen and build your testimony and act upon the principles you have studied.

What is a covenant? How are covenants made?

_____

_____

_____

_____

_____

_____

_____

_____

WE ARE DAUGHTERS OF OUR HEAVENLY FATHER

How will I remain pure and worthy to enter the temple to make sacred covenants?

_____

_____

_____

_____

_____

_____

_____

How do my covenants protect me from sin? When I break a covenant, how can I be made worthy again?

_____

_____

_____

_____

_____

_____

_____

Why do we make covenants?

_____

_____

_____

_____

_____

_____

_____

For further insight on the importance of covenant making and keeping, see Mosiah 18:8–11. See also:

- "Understanding Our Covenants with God," *Ensign*, July 2012;
- Henry B. Eyring, "Daughters in the Covenant," *Ensign*, May 2014;
- Rosemary M. Wixom, "Keeping Covenants Protects Us, Prepares Us, and Empowers Us," *Ensign*, May 2014;
- Ardeth G. Kapp, "'Crickets' Can Be Destroyed through Spirituality," *Ensign*, November 1990.

Chapter 19

RECEIVE THE
Ordinances
OF THE TEMPLE

RECEIVING YOUR ORDINANCES in the temple is the next step to your eternal progression. This is where you can perform the ordinances that make the binding and saving sacred covenants possible and real. In this most holy of places, you can receive the ordinances that bind you to God and to your family *forever*. That is a huge blessing!

How vital are temple ordinances to our salvation? Every person who has lived *must* have the ordinances to be able to return and live with Heavenly Father. Every person. Does that requirement seem a bit brash? A bit audacious? After all, there are billions and billions of people who have lived on the earth without having had the chance to hear about the restored gospel of Jesus Christ. Do we really believe this is the one and only path to return to His presence?

Yes, we do. And here is how it turns from being audacious to being beautifully caring. God wants every possible opportunity to have *all* of His children return home. In order to do this, they must receive the ordinances of the temple. Here is where the beauty comes in: the first time you go through the temple, you receive your own endowments. Every time after that, for the rest of your life, you are doing those exact same ordinances vicariously, or in behalf of those who did not have a chance to do them for themselves while they were alive. Just as we offer the gospel to others through missionary work, we offer saving ordinances to those who have passed on through our temple service.

Returning to the temple often, as our leaders have counseled, requires us to maintain a standard of purity and also provides a place to receive added inspiration in our own lives. This is a two-fold blessing that in turn keeps us progressing toward salvation while following His example of focusing our time and efforts on others through temple service. This outward focus is the essence of Christ's character.[1]

I hope you are feeling the magnitude of the importance of temples. They are quite literally our way back home and also our way to help others return back home.

In the Doctrine and Covenants, we find the capstone ordinances of the temple:

> And again . . . if a man marry a wife . . . by the new and everlasting covenant, and it is sealed unto them by the Holy Spirit of promise, . . . ye shall come forth in the first resurrection; . . . and shall inherit thrones, kingdoms, principalities, and powers, dominions, all heights and depths . . . [and] whatsoever my servant hath put upon them [the sealing power], in time, and through all eternity; and shall be of full force when they are out of the world. (D&C 132:19)

In other words, if you are sealed in the temple, you never have to say a permanent deathbed good-bye to those whom you hold most dear. That is the key, the golden ticket, to have your relationships last *forever.*

Here is an interesting thought: all of the ordinances leading up to the marriage sealing, we receive for ourselves, for our personal salvation. They are covenants we make between ourselves and God. The highest ordinance, the sealing ordinance, however, is truly an outwardly reaching covenant. We make this covenant not only with God, but also with our eternal partner. To truly achieve the highest degree of glory, we must be in a family unit. In fact, in the Guide to the Scriptures, we learn that the definition of eternal life is "to live forever *as families* in God's presence."[2]

We can look forward to receiving this highest saving ordinance, which binds us together in a family unit, to completely partake of eternal life according to God's plan. The marriage covenant is one of the greatest ways we can learn to become Christlike as we not only work for our own salvation but also learn to love and serve with our partner, to become one in purpose, and to keep those covenants that lead us back to God's presence.

Some of you may be thinking about what happens to those who, through no fault of their own, do not find someone with whom to make this most holy of covenants on earth. Our leaders have been quite clear on this matter, explaining that this life is certainly not the end of our progression and every worthy person will indeed have the opportunity to make that eternally significant covenant of marriage, whether in this life or the next.[3]

Doctrine and Covenants section 132 goes on to tell us that not only do we get to live forever with our family, but also "then shall they be gods, because they have no end; therefore shall they be from everlasting to everlasting, because they continue; then shall they be above all, because all things are subject unto them. Then shall they be gods, because they have all power, and the angels are subject unto them" (D&C 132:20).

We have the potential to become gods and goddesses. President Lorenzo Snow said, "As man now is, God once was: as God is now man may be."[4] Isn't that mind-boggling and yet simply beautiful?

Before you get too overwhelmed or offended by thinking that in becoming gods and goddesses we are going to replace God, pause and let's break it down. Consider this: What is the purpose of all parents regarding their children? Isn't it to raise them to one day be able to become good and wise parents themselves? Does my child becoming a parent lessen my parenthood by any measure? Absolutely not! I will always be my children's parent, just as my God will always be my God.

Now, if becoming parents and being able to raise children and live in families is of utmost importance for us here on earth, and if our time here is to help us prepare for our time after this life, wouldn't it stand to reason that what we are doing here would be "a type and a shadow of things which are to come" (Mosiah 13:10)? Our ability to eternally progress then becomes a natural extension of our growth here.

Set your sights on the temple. Do it now. Don't delay. And don't you ever budge. Whatever winds blow, whatever obstacles arise, don't lose sight of this eternally essential house of God.

POINTS TO PONDER FROM CHAPTER 19

You may choose to ponder and pray about each concept as you answer the questions below. Plan how you can strengthen and build your testimony and act upon the principles you have studied.

What ordinances have I completed for myself and what accompanying covenants have I made? What does the Lord expect me to do to honor these covenants? How am I doing in keeping them? How can I do better in honoring my covenants with God?

_____

_____

_____

_____

_____

_____

_____

_____

How does one prepare to enter the temple? What am I already doing, and what else can I do to do to prepare myself?

_____
_____
_____
_____
_____
_____
_____
_____

What do I need to change in myself to honor my divine nature and to be more worthy of the blessings of the temple?

_____
_____
_____
_____
_____
_____
_____
_____

What can I do to help my family live more worthily so we can receive the full blessings of the temple?

_____
_____
_____
_____
_____
_____
_____

What is the next ordinance I need to receive? How will I prepare to receive it?

_____
_____
_____
_____
_____
_____
_____
_____

For further insight on temple preparation, study Mosiah 2:6. See also:

- *Preparing to Enter the Holy Temple* (Salt Lake City: The Church of Jesus Christ of Latter-day Saints, 2002);
- Russell M. Nelson, "Personal Preparation for Temple Blessings," *Ensign*, May 2001.

Chapter 20

ENJOY THE
Blessings of
EXALTATION

"Ye cannot behold with your natural eyes, for the present time, the design of your God concerning those things which shall come hereafter, and the glory which shall follow after much tribulation." (D&C 58:3)

ES, YOU WILL have trials. Yes, you will have tribulations. Yes, you will have questions, and you may wonder about how you are going to get through certain challenges. But in the end, it is so worth the effort. We cannot even begin to imagine the greatness that our God, our Father in Heaven, has in store for us.

Let's go back again to the toothpick and yarn experiment. Remember that insignificant amount of space the toothpick takes up on the whole skein of yarn? That represents some understanding of the relative size of the trials you are now neck-deep in. And you will have the rest of eternity to rejoice with your Heavenly Father when you have made it through. Imagine that. A time when you can stand next to your Redeemer and say, "I did it." Or perhaps more aptly put, "We did it." You will have *all eternity* to rejoice and live in peace and joy—more happiness than you can possibly comprehend in this life.

And it all starts right here, right now. By *becoming* the Young Women theme, we are quite literally becoming beings who will be comfortable in His kingdom. Brad Wilcox explains, "Heaven will not be heaven for those who have not chosen to be heavenly."[1] You see, Heavenly Father doesn't only want us to be home, He wants us to be comfortable in that home. The theme says, "We will be prepared to . . . *enjoy* the blessings of exaltation" (emphasis added).

Yes, Heavenly Father and Jesus Christ want us to come back to Them to enjoy these precious blessings. In fact, throughout the scriptures, He pleads with us to come unto Him at least forty different times. My young sisters, He wants you to come to Him. And He doesn't need for you to be perfect to do so. Many of us are familiar with the promise in Isaiah about how our scarlet sins can be made "white as snow," that the crimson can "be as wool." Have you read the first phrase of that verse? It beautifully illustrates the love and grace of God: "Come now, and let us reason together, saith the Lord" (Isaiah 1:18). He's standing by, available to walk with you through the hard parts.

Can you feel His tender, loving voice calling out to you? Can you feel Him there, helping you along? Can you feel Him whispering, almost pleading with you, as He beckons you time and time again through scriptures, prophets, Church leaders, the Holy Ghost, and your parents to come unto Him (Matthew 11:28)? He so wants us to enjoy the blessings of exaltation. Do you believe that? Do you know He loves you? It is the entire reason He created this world. It is why He sent His Son. It is why Jesus drank the bitter cup and performed His perfect and eternal atoning sacrifice. All of that was done so you could enjoy the blessings of exaltation and live for an eternity in love and joy. Do you know that? Do you believe it? Do you live it? Sister Elaine Anderson Cannon, a former Young Women general president, stated, "There are two important days in a woman's life: The day she is born and the day she finds out why."[2]

You were put on this earth to gain a body, to be tested. But most important, you were put here to learn and grow so that you could go back home to heaven and truly enjoy all of the blessings of exaltation with your family by your side. And that truly is the greatest gift of all (D&C 14:7).

POINTS TO PONDER FROM CHAPTER 20

You may choose to ponder and pray about each concept as you answer the questions below. Plan how you can strengthen and build your testimony and act upon the principles you have studied.

What are the blessings of exaltation?

_____

_____

_____

_____

_____

_____

_____

Will I commit to do my best to be worthy to live in God's kingdom? How will I do this?

_____

_____

_____

_____

_____

_____

_____

How can I enjoy life now? Read D&C 24:8; 121. Are there other scriptures or talks from Church leaders that are helpful for me personally, especially in times of trial?

_____

_____

_____

_____

_____

_____

_____

_____

For further insight on exaltation and happiness, see 2 Nephi 2:25. See also:

- *Gospel Principles* (Salt Lake City: The Church of Jesus Christ of Latter-day Saints, 2011), 275–80;
- Thomas S. Monson, "Finding Joy in the Journey," *Ensign*, November 2008;
- Joseph B. Wirthlin, "Lessons Learned in the Journey of Life," *BYU Speeches*, November 7, 1999;
- Dieter F. Uchtdorf, "Of Regrets and Resolutions," *Ensign*, November 2012;
- Richard G. Scott, "Finding Joy in Life," *Ensign*, May 1996;
- Richard G. Scott, "Living a Life of Peace, Joy, and Purpose," *Ensign*, February 2014.

Chapter 21

PUTTING
It All
TOGETHER

WE HAVE BEEN on quite the journey together, you and I. We have traveled down the road beyond the words and right into the heart of the Young Women theme. I hope a complete picture is starting to come together for you, if it hasn't already. I really hope you are seeing the whole eternal vision open up in this beautiful Young Women theme that you review each week. One of the reasons you repeat it so often is to help you internalize the steps that will lead you to receive your ordinances in the temple and enjoy the blessings of exaltation with your family and Heavenly Father. The principles of standing as a witness and exemplifying the theme's values are the essence of our baptismal covenants, which set us firmly on the path to becoming like Christ—which is why we are here. Making sacred covenants empowers us with the blessings of the holy priesthood and is essential to our Father's plan of happiness. I love how the theme brings it all together, what we need to do and how to do it—the plan of salvation in a nutshell.

My young friend, you truly *are* a daughter of our Heavenly Father. I know He loves you. Do you love Him? I really think you do. You show that love by obeying His commandments and striving to mirror His image in your countenance (see Alma 5). I know in working to keep His commandments, you will stand strong and firm as a witness of Him at all times, in all things, and in all places. You can learn to accept and live the Young Women values through your daily decisions and your work as part of Personal Progress. Remember that as you choose to act upon these values, your testimony of their worth will grow.

I trust that you are doing much to strengthen your home and family now, and also to prepare to keep your future home and family strong and secure in a wayward world. I hope you are working to keep the covenants you made at baptism and are even now preparing to make those sacred covenants of the temple, where you will receive those eternally significant saving ordinances. Together, as we endure through all that life throws our way, we will always strive to live in a way that allows us, with our loved ones, to enjoy the blessings of exaltation.

You truly are a beloved, divine daughter of God. You were sent down here at this specific time, in your specific circumstance to fulfill all that God would have you do while on this earth.

The inspired Young Women theme can help you in so many ways. As you truly internalize its concepts, it will help you build a sure foundation, steadfast and immovable in Christ, so you don't have to rely on the whims of the world.

If you haven't yet, I would encourage you to decide now to learn, live, and grow to love each of the inspired phrases of this incredible theme. It will help you become a better woman, wife, mother, sister, aunt, friend, grandmother, and exalted daughter of our Heavenly Father.

Endnotes

CHAPTER 1: LET'S START AT THE BEGINNING

1. "Timeline of Young Women History," online edition. Accessed October 2013. https://www.lds.org/callings/young-women/leader-resources/history/timeline-of-young-women-history?lang=eng.

2. Ibid.

3. Personal phone interview with Ardeth G. Kapp, 10 January 2014. See also Anita Thompson, *Stand As A Witness* (Salt Lake City: Deseret Book, 2005), 275.

CHAPTER 2: WE ARE DAUGHTERS OF OUR HEAVENLY FATHER

1. Quorum of the Twelve Apostles, "Father, Consider Your Ways," *Ensign*, June 2002. Originally published as "A Message from The Church of Jesus Christ of Latter-day Saints," December 1973 pamphlet. Available online at https://www.lds.org/ensign/2002/06/father-consider-your-ways?lang=eng.

2. Brigham Young, *Journal of Discourses*, 4:268.

CHAPTER 3: WHO LOVES US

1. C. S. Lewis, *Mere Christianity*, Touchstone edition (New York: Touchstone, 1969), 147–48.

ENDNOTES

2. Robert McNamara, "Abraham Lincoln Quotations Everyone Should Know," *About Education*, online. Accessed July 18, 2014. http://history1800s.about.com/od/abrahamlincoln/a/lincolnquotes-01.htm.

3. David A. Bednar, "The Tender Mercies of the Lord," *Ensign*, May 2005, 99.

4. Ibid.

5. Dieter F. Uchtdorf, "Living the Gospel Joyful," *Ensign*, November 2014, 123; emphasis added.

CHAPTER 4: AND WE LOVE HIM

1. Marvin J. Ashton, "We Serve That Which We Love," *Ensign*, May 1981.

2. Dallin H. Oaks, "No Other Gods," *Ensign*, November 2013, 72.

3. Russell M. Nelson, "Let Your Faith Show," *Ensign*, May 2014, 29.

4. Ted Koppel, commencement speech at Duke University, 10 May 1987 (emphasis in original); quoted in Cecil O. Samuelson, "Those Things of Greatest Worth," BYU Speeches, April 25, 2013.

5. *For the Strength of Youth* (Salt Lake City: The Church of Jesus Christ of Latter-day Saints, 2011).

6. Dieter F. Uchtdorf, "The Love of God," *Ensign*, November 2009, 24.

7. Ibid., 22.

CHAPTER 5: WE WILL STAND AS WITNESSES OF GOD

1. See also David A. Bednar, "The Tender Mercies of the Lord," *Ensign*, May 2005, 99–101.

2. Thomas S. Monson, "Dare to Stand Alone," *Ensign*, November 2011, 60.

3. Margaret D. Nadauld, "Stand as a Witness," *Ensign*, May 2000.

4. James E. Faust, "The Light in Their Eyes," *Ensign*, November 2005, 20.

CHAPTER 6: AT ALL TIMES AND IN ALL THINGS, AND IN ALL PLACES

1. Jeffrey R. Holland, "Israel, Israel, God Is Calling," CES Devotional, St. George, UT, 9 September 2012.

2. Robert D. Hales, "Examples from the Life of a Prophet," *Ensign*, November 1981.

3. Margaret D. Nadauld, "Stand as a Witness," *Ensign*, May 2000; emphasis in original.

4. David A. Bednar, "Watching with All Perseverance," *Ensign*, May 2010, 42.

CHAPTER 7: AS WE STRIVE TO LIVE THE YOUNG WOMEN VALUES

1. "I Am a Child of God—Episode 25," *History of Hymns*, Mormon Channel, last updated February 21, 2012. Available online at http://www.mormonchannel.org/history-of-hymns/25. See also *Teachings of Presidents of the Church: Spencer W. Kimball* (Salt Lake City: The Church of Jesus Christ of Latter-day Saints, 2006), 1.

2. Lynn G. Robbins, "What Manner of Men and Women Ought Ye to Be?" *Ensign*, May 2011, 103.

CHAPTER 8: FAITH

1. "Faith," *Children's Songbook*, 96.

2. Spoken by the character of C. S. Lewis as portrayed in William Nicholson, *Shadowlands* (1989), 103; as quoted in Jean A.

Stevens, "'Fear Not; I Am with Thee,'" *Ensign*, May 2014, 82.

3. Russell M. Nelson, "Let Your Faith Show," *Ensign*, May 2014, 29.

4. Ibid.

5. Dieter F. Uchtdorf, "The Best Time to Plant a Tree," *Ensign*, January 2014, 6.

6. Neal A. Maxwell, *That Ye May Believe* (Salt Lake City: Bookcraft, 1992), 84. Quoted in Cory H. Maxwell, ed., *The Neal A. Maxwell Quote Book* (Salt Lake City: Bookcraft, 1997).

7. Ezra Taft Benson, "The Book of Mormon Is the Word of God," *Ensign*, January 1988.

8. Neil L. Andersen, "Trial of Your Faith," *Ensign*, November 2012, 41.

9. Ibid., 49.

10. Dieter F. Uchtdorf, "Come, Join with Us," *Ensign*, November 2013, 23.

11. Quoted in Truman G. Madsen, *The Highest in Us* (Salt Lake City: Bookcraft, 1978), 49.

CHAPTER 9: DIVINE NATURE

1. Frank Bajak, "Is this man the oldest living person on record?" *USA Today*, last modified 14 August 2013. Available online at http://www.usatoday.com/story/news/world/2013/08/14/bolivia-oldest-man/2656247/.

2. Dieter F. Uchtdorf, "You Matter to Him," *Ensign*, November 2011, 20.

3. Ibid.

4. Ibid, 22.

5. Gordon B. Hinckley, "Rise to the Stature of the Divine within You," *Ensign*, November 1989.

CHAPTER 11: KNOWLEDGE

1. Gordon B. Hinckley, "Our Responsibility to Our Young Women," *Ensign*, September 1988.

2. See "Be Thou Humble," *Hymns*, no. 130.

3. Brad Wilcox, "His Grace Is Sufficient," *BYU Speeches*, 12 July 2011.

4. "Respectfully Quoted," Bartleby.com, accessed May 2015. Available online at http://www.bartleby.com/73/1225.html.

5. "Mother's Day Quotes," Ancestry.com, accessed May 2014. Available online at http://homepages.rootsweb.ancestry.com/~homespun/mdquotes.html.

6. Russell M. Nelson, "Youth of the Noble Birthright: What Will You Choose?" CES Devotional, 6 September 2013; emphasis added.

7. *For the Strength of Youth* (Salt Lake City: The Church of Jesus Christ of Latter-day Saints, 2011), 9.

8. Gordon B. Hinckley, "Rise to the Stature of the Divine within You," *Ensign*, November 1989.

9. *Teachings of Presidents of the Church: Brigham Young* (Salt Lake City: The Church of Jesus Christ of Latter-day Saints, 1997), 195.

10. See also N. Eldon Tanner, "The Laws of God," *Ensign*, November 1975.

11. Spencer W. Kimball, "The Role of Righteous Women," *Ensign*, November 1979. Available online at https://www.lds.org/ensign/1979/11/the-role-of-righteous-women?lang=eng

CHAPTER 12: CHOICE AND ACCOUNTABILITY

1. Thomas S. Monson, "The Three Rs of Choice," *Ensign*, November 2010, 67.

ENDNOTES

2. *Teachings of Presidents of the Church: David O. McKay* (Salt Lake City: The Church of Jesus Christ of Latter-day Saints, 2011), 208.

3. Marvin J. Ashton, "A Pattern in All Things," *Ensign*, November 1990.

4. D. Todd Christofferson, "Free Forever, to Act for Themselves," *Ensign*, November 2014.

5. Richard G. Scott, "Jesus Christ, Our Redeemer," *Ensign*, May 1997.

6. Lex De Azevedo, "Choosing," *My Turn on Earth* (Excel Entertainment, 1997), CD.

7. James E. Faust, "'The Great Imitator,'" *Ensign*, November 1987.

8. Sheri Dew, *No One Can Take Your Place* (Salt Lake City: Deseret Book, 2004), 20.

9. Mervyn B. Arnold, "What Have You Done with My Name?" *Ensign*, November 2010, 106.

10. Thomas S. Monson, "The Three Rs of Choice," *Ensign*, November 2010, 68.

11. Gordon B. Hinckley, "Watch the Switches in Your Life," *Ensign*, January 1973.

12. Thomas S. Monson, "The Three Rs of Choice," *Ensign*, November 2010, 67.

13. Dallin H. Oaks, "Where Will It Lead?" *BYU Speeches*, 9 November 2004.

14. Jeffrey R. Holland, "We Are All Enlisted," *Ensign*, November 2011, 45.

15. Ibid.

16. Quoted in Bruce K. Satterfield, "Teachings Concerning the Kingdom of God," class handout. Available online at http://emp.byui.edu/satterfieldb/PDF/Quotes/Kingdom%20of%20God.pdf.

17. Richard C. Edgley, "The Rescue for Real Growth," *Ensign*, May 2012, 53.

18. Richard G. Scott, "Personal Strength through the Atonement of Jesus Christ," *Ensign*, November 2013, 84.

19. Jeffrey R. Holland, "The Laborers in the Vineyard," *Ensign*, May 2012, 33.

CHAPTER 13: GOOD WORKS

1. Robert C. Gay, "What Shall a Man Give in Exchange for His Soul?" *Ensign*, November 2012, 35.

2. Thomas S. Monson, "Finding Joy in the Journey," *Ensign*, November 2008, 86.

3. Chieko Okazaki, "Spit and Mud and Kigatsuku," *Ensign*, May 1992.

4. M. Russell Ballard, "Be Anxiously Engaged," *Ensign*, November 2012, 29.

5. "Honey Bee Trivia," York County Beekeepers' Association, accessed 23 May 2014. Available online at http://www.ycbk.org/beetrivia.html.

6. Spencer W. Kimball, "The Abundant Life," *Ensign*, July 1978.

7. Gordon B. Hinckley, "Words of the Prophet: Put Your Shoulder to the Wheel," *New Era*, July 2000.

CHAPTER 14: INTEGRITY

1. Joseph B. Wirthlin, "Priceless Integrity," *New Era*, July 1994.

2. Quoted in James E. Faust, "The Light in Their Eyes," *Ensign*, November 2005, 20.

3. Clayton M. Christensen, James Allworth, and Karen Dillon, *How Will You Measure Your Life?* (New York: HarperCollins, 2012), 189–90.

4. Personal phone interview with Ardeth G. Kapp, 10 January 2014. See also Anita Thompson, *Stand As A Witness* (Salt Lake City: Deseret Book, 2005), 271.

CHAPTER 15: VIRTUE

1. Elaine S. Dalton, "A Return to Virtue," *Ensign*, November 2008, 78–79.

2. Letter to General Authorities; Area Seventies; Stake, Mission, and District Presidents; Bishops and Branch Presidents from the First Presidency, 28 November 2008. Quoted in "Virtue Added as Young Women Value," *Ensign*, February 2009.

3. Quoted in Heather Whittle Wrigley, "Changing the World One Virtuous Woman at a Time," *Ensign*, January 2010, 74–75.

4. Elaine S. Dalton, "A Return to Virtue," *Ensign*, November 2008, 78.

5. *Preach My Gospel* (Salt Lake City: The Church of Jesus Christ of Latter-day Saints, 2004), 118.

6. Elaine S. Dalton, "A Return to Virtue," *Ensign*, November 2008, 79.

7. Ibid.

8. Lena Jensen, "Virtue," 31 March 1884, accessed 23 November 2013. IP information for the Young Ladies Advocate, Moroni Ward, Sanpete Stake, 1884–1885 (CHL call number LR 5786 21).

9. "Adolescent Sexual Behavior: Demographics," Advocates for Youth, last updated February 2012. Available online at http://www.advocatesforyouth.org/component/content/article/413-adolescent-sexual-behavior-i-demographics.

10. Gordon B. Hinckley, "Life's Obligations," *Ensign*, February 1999.

11. Bruce R. McConkie, "Agency or Inspiration—Which?" *BYU Speeches*, 27 February 1973.

12. See "Sexual Purity," *For the Strength of Youth* (Salt Lake City: The Church of Jesus Christ of Latter-day Saints, 2011).

13. D. Todd Christofferson, "The Moral Force of Women," *Ensign*, November 2013, 29.

14. Ibid.

15. "Who are the Victims?" *RAINN*, last modified 2009, accessed May 2015. Available online at https://www.rainn.org/get-information/statistics/sexual-assault-victims.

16. "Self-Blame and Shame," *Rape Treatment Center*, accessed May 2015. Available online at http://www.911rape.org/impact-of-rape/self-blame-and-shame.

17. Tracy Jarrett, "'I was broken beyond repair': Elizabeth Smart recalls kidnapping ordeal," NBC News, last modified October 5, 2013, accessed May 2015. Available online at http://www.nbcnews.com/news/other/i-was-broken-beyond-repair-elizabeth-smart-recalls-kidnapping-ordeal-f8C11336267.

18. Elizabeth Smart, "About Elizabeth Smart," Facebook, accessed November 1, 2014. Available online at https://www.facebook.com/pages/Elizabeth-Smart/202000139856379#.

19. Ann F. Pritt, "Healing the Spiritual Wounds of Sexual Abuse," *Ensign*, April 2001, 61.

20. See "Abuse," *Gospel Topics*, LDS.org, accessed November 1, 2014. Available online at https://www.lds.org/topics/abuse?lang=eng.

21. Quoted in Heather Whittle Wrigley, "Changing the World One Virtuous Woman at a Time," *Ensign*, January 2010.

CHAPTER 16: WE BELIEVE AS WE COME TO ACCEPT AND ACT UPON THESE VALUES

1. Elaine S. Dalton, "A Return to Virtue," *Ensign*, November 2008, 80.

2. Quoted in Elaine S. Dalton, "A Return to Virtue," *Ensign*, November 2008, 80.

CHAPTER 17: WE WILL BE PREPARED TO STRENGTHEN HOME AND FAMILY

1. Personal phone interview with Margaret D. Nadauld, 4 February 2014.

2. "The Family: A Proclamation to the World," *Ensign*, November 1995, 102.

3. Charles Duhigg, *The Power of Habit: Why We Do What We Do in Life and Business* (New York: Random House, 2012), 109.

4. Jon Hittinger, "Plato and Aristotle on the Family and the *Polis*," *The Saint Anselm Journal* 8.2, Spring 2013, University of St. Thomas, Houston, online edition. Available at http://www.anselm.edu/Documents/Institute%20for%20Saint%20Anselm%20Studies/spring%202013/Hittinger,%20The%20family%20and%20the%20polis.pdf.

5. William Bennett, "Stronger Families, Stronger Societies." *New York Times*. April 24, 2014, online edition. Available at http://www.nytimes.com/roomfordebate/2012/04/24/are-family-values-outdated/stronger-families-stronger-societies.

6. The Witherspoon Institute, *Marriage and the Public Good: Ten Principles* (Princeton, New Jersey: The Witherspoon Institute, 2008), 9–10. Online edition. Available at http://protectmarriage.com/wp-content/uploads/2012/11/WI_Marriage.pdf.

7. Ibid., 13.

8. Robert J. Sampson, "Unemployment and Imbalanced Sex Ratios: Race Specific Consequences for Family Structure and Crime," in M. B. Tucker and C. Mitchell-Kernan, eds., *The Decline in Marriage among African Americans* (New York: Russell Sage Foundation, 1995), 249. As quoted in *Marriage and the Public Good: Ten Principles* (Princeton, New Jersey: The Witherspoon Institute, 2008), 16.

9. See Jeffrey R. Holland, "Motherhood: An Eternal Partnership with God," LDS.org, accessed May 2014. Available at https://www.lds.org/pages/motherhood.

10. Quoted in *Daughters in My Kingdom: The History and Work of Relief Society* (Salt Lake City: The Church of Jesus Christ of Latter-day Saints, 2011), 145.

11. Ibid., 148–49.

12. Google Dictionary, "Definition of Guardian," accessed February 2014. Available at https://www.google.com/#q= definition+of+guardian.

CHAPTER 18: MAKE AND KEEP SACRED COVENANTS

1. Ardeth G. Kapp, "'Crickets' Can Be Destroyed through Spirituality," *Ensign*, November 1990.

2. Linda K. Burton, "The Power, Joy, and Love of Covenant Keeping," *Ensign*, November 2013, 111.

3. Dieter F. Uchtdorf, "Are You Sleeping through the Restoration?" *Ensign*, May 2014, 61.

CHAPTER 19: RECEIVE THE ORDINANCES OF THE TEMPLE

1. David A. Bednar, *Act in Doctrine* (Salt Lake City: Deseret Book, 2012).

2. The Guide to the Scriptures, "Eternal Life," LDS.org, http:// www.lds.org/scriptures/gs/eternal-life?lang=eng.

3. Spencer W. Kimball, "The Importance of Celestial Marriage," *Ensign*, October 1979, 5.

4. Quoted in *Teachings of Presidents of the Church: Lorenzo Snow* (Salt Lake City: The Church of Jesus Christ of Latter-day Saints, 2012), 83.

ENDNOTES

CHAPTER 20: ENJOY THE BLESSINGS OF EXALTATION

1. Brad Wilcox, "His Grace Is Sufficient," *BYU Speeches*, 12 July 2011.

2. Elaine Anderson Cannon, "'Let Me Soar,' Women Counseled," *Church News*, 17 October 1981, 3. Quoted in "Presidents of the Young Women Organization through the Years," *Ensign*, June 2008.

About the Author

Jen Brewer got her degree in dietetics from BYU, married a handsome hunk of a husband, and spent the next ten years traipsing around the country with him as he pursued a medical degree, while adding children to their ever-growing family. They have now settled in Minnesota, where she works full time as a mother of seven, as well as pursues her passions of nutrition education, speaking to the youth, and writing. She speaks often to various groups of all ages. Her passion is reaching out to the youth and helping them see their true potential in the kingdom of God. She is a popular speaker at Education Week Youth Track at BYU–Idaho, as well as at stakes and wards all over the country.